CRISIS OF SOCIALISM—
Notes in Defence of a Commitment—Vol. 5

CONTEMPORARY ECOLOGICAL CRISIS

A Marxist View

CRISIS OF SOCIALISM—
Notes in Defence of a Commitment—Vol. 5

CONTEMPORARY ECOLOGICAL CRISIS

A Marxist View

Randhir Singh

AAKAR

Contemporary Ecological Crisis—A Marxist View
Randhir Singh

First Published 2009
Reprinted 2020

ISBN 978-81-89833-92-3 (Pb)

Published by
AAKAR BOOKS
28 E Pocket IV, Mayur Vihar Phase I
Delhi 110 091, India
www.aakarbooks.com

Printed at
Sapra Brothers, Noida

Contents

Publisher's Note 7
Author—In Lieu of a Biodata 9
Preface to the Original Edition 19
Ecological Crisis and Future of Socialism 27
Index 153

Publisher's Note

Professor Randhir Singh's *Crisis of Socialism—Notes in Defence of a Commitment* (xiii+1087 pages) was originally published by Ajanta Books International in 2006. A response to the collapse of Soviet Union's 'actually existing socialism' and dealing with the basic issues of why and how of this collapse, its implications and where it leaves the question of socialism in our time, the book has been hailed as a pioneering work—'one of the most important, if not *the* most important book we have ever read', 'a key to all that is going on in our world today', 'if there were a required reading list for the U.S. left, this should be on it', and so on—and there has been a persistent demand for its argument to be available in a form easier to handle and access. Therefore, with the consent of the author and in consultation with him, we at Aakar Books have decided to publish it as a thematically reorganized 6 volume edition : Volume I (Chapter 2 and 3, titled **Of Marxism and Socialism** — also available in the author's **Marxism, Socialism, Indian Politics—A View from the Left,** published by us); Volume II (Prologue, Chapters 1, 4, 5, 6, 7, 8, 9, 11, 12, 13 and Epilogue, titled **What was built and What failed in the Soviet Union);** Volume III (Chapters 10, 14, 15, 16, titled **The World after the Soviet Collapse);** Volume IV (Chapters 18 and 19, titled **The Right Lesson and The Wrong Conclusion);** Volume V (Chapter 20, titled **Contemporary Ecological Crisis—A Marxist View);** Volume VI (Chapter 21 and 22, titled **Struggle for Socialism—Some Issues).**

—K.K. Saxena

In Lieu of a Biodata*

There is a certain inevitability about it. Sooner or later someone was bound to ask me, again, for my biodata.

A 'biodata', now, has been a source of perennial embarrassment for me. For I simply don't have any—I have no credentials at all so far as scholarship in the academy goes. I have only a life to speak of, lived somewhat differently, and on a generous interpretation, maybe a little more meaningfully too. Here, very sketchily, then, is some of the more public part of the story, for whatever it is worth.

Childhood, they say, is important, always and in many ways. For me it was a rather unhappy childhood, very bleak and altogether lonely. I literally lived and survived on books, which partly explains my lifelong love for and involvement with them. This childhood, possibly, also left me with a certain sensitivity for the reality of suffering in the human condition of our time.

Over this childhood loomed large the heroic figure of Bhagat Singh. A morning is still vividly etched on my mind, the morning after he and his comrades were hanged. I was detained, briefly, while passing in front of the Lahore Central Jail on my way to the Borstal primary school in the neighbourhood. The army and the police, a surging sea of

---

* An 'autobiographical note' written in response to a request for biodata for a felicitation volume (1988).

humanity, tears in each eye and the proud faces, portraits, of the martyrs everywhere—and the defiant unending cry of '*Inquilab zindabad*'.... That morning was born a dream which, I believe, in some form or the other, has always stayed with me. Years later I was to spend a few months, among the happiest in my life, in the 'Terrorist Ward' of this very prison with some of the surviving comrades of Bhagat Singh—Kishori Lal and others—who had in the meantime joined the Communist Party.

Thus I grew up. And in due course, on the eve of the Second World War, I again came to Lahore, this time for my studies at a college there. My father, a remarkable man in his own mixed sort of way—a brilliant physician and surgeon, profoundly religious and puritanical, with a rather deadly combination of Gandhi and Lenin in his head—sensing the turbulence inside me, his only son, had advised: 'Do anything out there but don't join some illegal organisation'. Predictably, this was the first thing I did on reaching Lahore. Even as I was searching for it, the Communist Party found me. When my father admonished me that I had shown scant regard for the family, I wrote back: 'I have found my real family'. The Communist Party meant this and very much more in those days, to many of us at least. Besides, there was a certain pride in being a Communist. I still remember from those times two lines from the poet C. Day Lewis. A question and an answer, they went something like this:

> Why do we on seeing a Red feel small?
> For he is future walking to meet us—

Fifty years later, badly buffeted, some of this pride yet remains. Incidentally, this is also how I came to Marxism—beginning with whatever Marxism was then available with the Comintern and permitted or possible in our country under the British rule.

Followed years of hectic activity in the students' movement and in the underground with the Communist Party, including entire vacations spent with workers in factories away from Lahore or with peasants in their villages.

We were good students, among the best in the University. I duly qualified for admission to the Medical College. But it was clear that the demands of ever-increasing political work would be impossible to reconcile with those of a study in medicine. I decided to shift to a 'soft' discipline. I was advised that Political Science was, possibly, the easiest subject to get your master's degree in. That, perhaps, is one reason why I could never take it seriously. Later I was to discover that it is also, possibly, the poorest among the social sciences. And if I may suggest, one important reason for its poverty as a social scientific enterprise is its near-universal ignorance of or hostility towards Marxism as social science; though, in recent years, it has not been averse to recognising Marxism as 'political thought'.

Be that as it may, in a couple of years even the pursuit of Political Science had to be given up for full-time work with the Communist Party—on the party wage of, I think, rupees twenty or twenty-five per month. For most of the next five years and more, till after the Partition, I moved around the villages and towns of Punjab, organising people and persuading them to move through their struggle for freedom towards a social revolution in this country, which I believe still needs to be made.

Soon enough I landed in prison, charged with opposition to 'the war effort' of the British Government in India. (Incidentally, it was 'the people's war' period!) Released, after nearly a year's imprisonment, I was for some time put under the usual restrictions on movement, meetings, etc. I filled up the time with a stint on the editorial staff of the Party's Punjabi weekly, *Jang-i-Azadi*. I also started work on a biography of the still active legendary revolutionary, Baba Gurmukh Singh, a fragment of which was later published as *Ghadar Heroes: A Forgotten Story of the Punjab Revolutionaries of 1914-1915* (1945). My professor at the University—he was none other than Dr. J.N. Khosla—who was rather fond of me, insisted that I use this opportunity to at least finish my studies. The Party gave me the required leave for a couple of months, and my professor provided me with the necessary certificate of attendance at classes—which partly overlapped the period I was in prison! I duly took the examination—and was soon back in the villages.

(The degree, a first-class-first, was to come in very handy later in my life, at Delhi.)

Came the great popular struggles, the near-revolutionary upsurge of the mid-1940s, the haggling and compromising presided over by Imperialism, the consequent riots, the Partition, and more riots—and Indian independence. A faith had been kept *and* betrayed. Those were glorious yet ignominy-laden years, the years at once of victory and defeat for the Indian people. More specifically, it was the final success, however ambiguous, of a Gandhi and bourgeois-led politics, and a definitive failure, only temporary we thought, of our Communist politics, which included that last adventurist flourish with B.T.R. as well as the heroic struggle in Telengana. One lived, shared and fought through it all—and survived. Some of this experience, intensely personal as well as political and collective, found expression in a small collection of poems in Punjabi—*Rahan Di Dhoor* (1950). In one of these, I recorded:

> A caravan has reached the destination,
> And yet lost its way—

I never wrote poetry again—don't ask me why. Only very recently I have learnt that early in 1951 itself, a distinguished critic had, in a review, hailed my book as a truly significant piece of work. A contemporary scholar even considers it to be the best poetry of that period, though, as he told me, he had difficulty in locating its author!

It would appear that, as in scholarship, so in poetry, and may be in much else besides, I am a genuine 'might have been'.

I came to Delhi sometime after the Partition, having lived with death the previous few months and on the way. Uprooted, a refugee, everything around me, including my politics in a shambles, I sought a new foothold in life—only temporarily, I had then thought, mistakenly. I started teaching at what was then known as Camp College, an institution set up by the Punjab University at Delhi for refugee students and teachers. Even as I began to enjoy my new vocation, the Party, passing through a series of crises, both internal and external, finally opted for 'peaceful', 'parliamentary' ways. And so it came to pass, with other tangible and not-so-tangible factors contributing, that, over a period of time—during which I still edited from Delhi its theoretical monthly in Punjabi, *Sada Jug* (till removed, charged with 'individualism' and 'intellectual arrogance' for refusing to publish a BTR criticism of Mao Tse-tung), and translated *Communist Manifesto* and some more Marx into Punjabi—I just opted out of the Party. [Later, soon after its formation, I was to spend a few years in the Communist Party (Marxist)]. For me the comforting rationalisation was that in our society, after 'revolution-making', teaching perhaps holds the maximum possibilities for a non-alienated life. Here, if you want, but only if you *want*, earning your living can be at the same time living your life. So teaching it was to be for me for the rest of my life. Soon I moved from Camp College to Delhi College, where I was to teach for nearly two decades; then, after a brief stint at Jawaharlal Nehru University, in 1972 I joined Delhi University, rather late in life, as Professor of Political Theory.

Thus it is that having spent some of the best years of my life elsewhere, away from the academy, and the rest only teaching, scholarship has simply passed me by. Hence, as I said in the beginning, 'biodata' has been a perennial embarrassment —for I never managed to acquire one as a scholar. I have no research degrees and no publications except some odd entirely casual exercises, including the book, *Reason, Revolution and Political Theory*, which was an ad hoc response to a provocation in the classroom when my students wanted me to explain and defend an observation I had made. I have had no string of scholars working 'under' me, no fellowships, no research projects, no study or other academic leaves, no 'seminaring', national or international, nothing—not even a visit abroad that has come to certify any sort of achievement or standing as a scholar these days!

Recently, the Indian Council of Social Science Research, perhaps wanting to be helpful, more than once extended me invitations involving 'a foreign visit' each time. Having somehow missed or evaded every such opportunity or activity in the past, I thought, I would make a virtue of it—and declined. Besides, it seemed a bit too late in life for me to now get started on this. Perhaps I also wanted to make certain that there is at least one professor in this country who has not been abroad!

Incidentally, the Council have also very generously offered me a National Fellowship which I have accepted. So I may yet end up as a scholar, though, I am not too sure. For the subject on which I have chosen to write a brief monograph is rather away from what have been my major concerns as a teacher—Western Political Thought, Contemporary Political Theory, Marxism. My subject is so obviously *political*, not 'scholarly'; I seek an understanding of Indian politics which may, it is hoped, help towards 'a more effective people's intervention in what is happening in our country'. What is more, contrary to the current fashions in the world of Marxian scholarship, where 'orthodoxy' is almost a dirty word, and a comfortable and comforting 'post-Marxism' is abroad, I visualise my work as an exercise in Marxist orthodoxy!

If I have, most of the time, done none of the things that scholars are normally supposed to do, I have been, most of the time, busy with what they are normally supposed to keep away from. Which is as well, for life has been such fun this way. I have thus functioned, in the profession and in the university, more as a militant on the Left—even when revising the syllabi in Political Science whenever or wherever I got the opportunity to do so, or putting in a rather noisy plea on behalf of Political Theory in general and Marxism in particular on the campuses of Indian universities. As a militant, the aim was always *hegemony* and not factional or mere economic or organisational gains.

Over the years, teaching and related work apart, I have, along with many others of course, spent a great deal of time helping build up the teachers' movement, fighting for democratic rights and reforms in the university (with the vice-chancellors and against them), carrying on socialist education among workers, students and teachers, including school-teachers, running Marx Clubs and putting together Socialist Groups (one such effort, incidentally, went into the making of the Communist Party (Marxist) on Delhi University campus), writing and publishing pamphlets and bulletins, editing and producing, distributing or circulating journals like *Enquiry, Socialist Digest, The Marxist Review, Monthly Review, Science and Society* and *New Left Review*, campaigning on issues like Vietnam and Czechoslovakia, collecting signatures for Iranian students and others, mobilising and marching for all sorts of popular causes, associating with almost any radical initiative on the campus and every revolutionary venture off it, an association which on occasions, quite understandably, even ended in a love–hate relationship, —and so on. That is how it has been for the most part over nearly forty long years.

But if scholarship has passed me by, I have not done too badly as a teacher. At least that is what my students, colleagues, and many others tell me. And I am inclined to believe them; maybe because I very much want to. I have taught in the departments of History, Political Science, and occasionally Philosophy. Students have come to my classes from other disciplines and other universities, from Economics and Sociology, Law and Literature, Mathematics, even Chemistry and Physics. (Perhaps Commerce and Business Management alone have been missing!) And they have given me abundantly of their love and affection, and thoughtful appreciation. This has been compensation enough for whatever I may have missed out on not being a scholar. It was compensation enough especially during periods of bitter conflict and controversy which, inevitably, have been a persistent feature of my long career as a teacher. It is the students who first spoke of 'a legend in Delhi University'. And it is, above all, to them that I trace the real source of an observation Bertell Ollman has made, though it is also expressive of his own characteristic generosity. After his recent visit to Delhi and Jawaharlal Nehru Universities, he writes: 'If I wasn't already over 50, I would probably say something like: when I grow up I want to be a Professor like Randhir Singh.' Yes, teaching has been compensation enough.

At one of the farewell meetings at Delhi University, they questioned me on the subject of my teaching. I responded that, given the 'functional rationality' governing the organised structures of teaching and research, so that scholarly writing is increasingly addressed not to problems or publics but to peers and to prestige and preferment in the needlessly bureaucratised academic professions, and given the growing, and often mindless, specialisation in the social sciences (including Political Science) which is resulting in a situation where fewer and fewer people are hearing more and more about less and less—given all this, a certain lack of conventional academic scholarship can even be an advantage in that it may help one see the social reality as a whole, see the wood and not just the trees, and thus address, as teacher or scholar (or activist), the real problems of society.

Incidentally, I also told them, my students and colleagues, that, for one speaking up for Marxism, my knowledge of Economics is shockingly poor and that I have always regretted it. But this lack, perhaps, has made me that much more sensitive to the humanist, philosophical, and above all political dimensions of Marxism. Of course, I added that 'politics as revolution' is central to Marxism, at least to Marxism as Karl Marx practised it. 'Marx was before all else a revolutionist', as Engels put it.

These are, however, somewhat peripheral considerations. I had gone on to suggest that its strictly academic aspects apart, my teaching could be viewed as a form of 'robinhooding' which, even as it functions within the system, yet seeks to stretch it to its limits. Of course, this 'robinhooding', this functioning as a radical or a Marxist inside the classroom, has its problems and its risks too. The most important problem is that it needs to have a certain quality about it which, above all, demands a genuine and acknowledged familiarity with the mainstream scholarship in the concerned field or discipline, one's reservations about it notwithstanding. Lacking this, it can easily degenerate into vulgar propaganda or empty moral rhetoric. As a student coming from the discipline of English literature, in a complementary reference, once said: 'One needs to have that rare combination of idealism and intelligence.' As for the risks, the most important ones concern the security of job and the denial of promotion. I must admit that I have been rather lucky in this regard. It is true that whenever interviewed, the selection committees invariably turned me down. Yet appointments came, by invitation, including the professorship in 1972, when, incidentally, seeing everyone making a beeline for Jawaharlal Nehru University, I chose instead to opt for the University of Delhi.

'Robinhooding' has its minor risks also. For me it has meant another continuous struggle from the day I started teaching. At the very outset they asked for an undertaking 'not to teach subversion'. Later, they stopped you, again and again, from teaching, or teaching a particular course. For long years, they would let me teach only Plato and not Marx—so that you learn to teach Marx via Plato, which is not only possible but is in some ways far more effective also, for obvious reasons. They can organise harassment and humiliation for you in diverse ways, with the lumpen elements in the academic community thrown in.... One has struggled against all this and *them* all along, and with a reasonable measure of success. My only regret is for the students and teachers who, now and then, had to suffer for their association with me.

There are problems and there are risks. And for better credibility here one must learn to say 'no' to at least some of the innumerable benefits, the cooptive attractions the system has to offer even to a radical teacher, though this 'no' is only of symbolic value. But the most important thing is to be aware of the limitations, even ambiguities, inherent in the very nature of 'robinhooding' as an academic exercise. And for this reason one needs to be very modest about what one is doing or achieving here.

What is more, in so far as it is an exercise *within* the system, it is always in danger of itself becoming a form of cooption into it. In fact, the more you succeed in what you are doing, the more you are also, in an important sense, lending legitimacy to the system as a whole. Such is the dialectics implicit in this mode or style of teaching. That is why its quality is of decisive importance. Even so, how effective it is in its own modest manner, and how it contributes to any qualitative departures in the system, will be determined by other, larger social forces at work in the historical process in this country. We can only recognise and try to help these in whatever way we can.

I will only add that what goes on within the discipline of Political Science or its classrooms, or, for that matter, within the universities and the social science institutes of this country, is only of marginal relevance to the problems and prospects of the Indian people's struggle for a better future. But this is where we work—teachers, students, scholars, all others. And it is axiomatic, for most of us, that we make our efforts where we work, or we shall make no effort at all.

Preface to the Original Edition

This is a book which ought to have been published more than a decade back when its argument was first delivered as a series of lectures in memory of my friend and political associate Professor Moin Shakir at Marathwada University, Aurangabad, in February 1991. The writing naturally bears its mark but the delay has taken nothing away from the validity or relevance of my argument.

I had spoken from detailed notes and was supposed to produce a written version of these lectures. Associated with the communist movement for more than half a century, and mindful of Moin Shakir's concerns, I proceeded to write them down as a militant's response to what had happened in the Soviet Union, addressed to fellow militants in the movement and radicals at large. Part of what I wrote was published from time to time in the following years. The opening section was published in 1992 itself – in *Economic and Political Weekly* – entitled 'Crisis of Socialism – Notes in Defence of a Commitment'. This piece of writing, conveying something of my 'journey through communism' since 1939, was much noticed and appreciated at home and abroad and was reproduced and translated in many places, including an Urdu journal in Pakistan. Victor G. Kiernan, the distinguished historian, called it a 'splendid article'. Paul Sweezy and Harry Magdoff were equally appreciative. Sweezy noticed its appeal for readers of *Monthly Review* – 'many of whom (perhaps too many!) have been through similar experiences in their own lives' – and wrote to me: 'I read the piece with great interest and found it both eloquent and moving. Different as our experiences have been during the last half century, there is still much we have in common in reacting to the collapse of the revolutionary experiment in which and for which we had such high hopes'. This article soon came to be viewed as a document of the times. I have included it here as a *Prologue* to the book.

I had begun writing this draft but could not, or did not, complete it for reasons as diverse as my diffidence or lack of discipline when it comes to writing things down, more pressing or welcome academic engagements or political work, bouts of personal ill-health and, not the least, the hassles and harassments of ordinary middle class existence in the corrupt, communalised and mafiaised polity that much of India is today. The most important reason, however, was my awareness that scholars far more competent than me were writing on the subject, making it unnecessary for me to carry out the essentially secondary exercise of putting on paper what I had said at Aurangabad. And I was not wrong. We have since, for example, lstvan Meszaros' magisterial *Beyond Capital – Towards a Theory of Transition,* which has been rightly assessed as 'the definitive Marxian synthesis for the present moment, the phase of what Meszaros calls capital's *structural crisis'*. I have myself found it most useful for my argument in several places while completing these notes.

I however kept speaking on the subject or its sub-themes, discussing them with radical groups, at universities and other formal and informal gatherings; and pressure kept mounting, as much from the old-generation friends of socialism as from the new crop of young activists, that I put down my argument, such as it is, in writing. A National Fellowship at the Institute of Advanced Study, Shimla, finally persuaded me to take the plunge. But for this fellowship I would have made no progress at all with the completion of these notes. But the unexplained termination of this fellowship proved equally disruptive and delayed the completion of even this first draft by a few years. The writing is therefore obviously flawed in many ways. It bears the mark of being written, or completed, in bits, over a long period of time. That its sub-themes were the subject of separate treatment or lectures at different times or places has also contributed to uneven writing and to repetition in parts of the book. The format of Notes, with its need to provide the context of and complete the specific point being made has also added to the problem of repetition. I had expected my student and friend Arvind N. Das to take care of all this, edit and put this draft in proper shape for publication. But his premature death ruled this out. I thought of doing the needful myself, but somehow this has not been possible. In the meantime, the publication of some parts in the weekly *Mainstream* had created a constituency for what I have to say. The desirability of a better organized, more rigorously argued, and linguistically felicitous book notwithstanding, there was a growing demand that these notes be published, as they are – in their present rough form, even without references or footnotes – without any further delay. S. Balwant at the Ajanta Books International having agreed to do so, I, for myself, can only seek reader's indulgence, ask her or him to bear with the many inadequacies of this publication. What is important or really matters is its basic argument.

Occasional use of my earlier writings, particularly *Reason, Revolution and Political Theory* apart, these notes are based on my necessarily limited reading, rather what I remembered of it. I have borrowed freely from other scholars, taken their analyses as my own, used their arguments, at times in their own words, and not hesitated to quote them at length for the simple reason that they had expressed the idea or the argument better than I could have done. My debts are far too many to be acknowledged. Those familiar with the literature will easily recognize them. For me it is enough to rationalize it all by saying that these are scholars who are, so to speak, more or less on my side of the barricades.

There is one debt, however, which I would still like to explicitly acknowledge – to *Monthly Review*. It is the journal I have felt most comfortable with, intellectually and politically, over the past 50 odd years, and my debt here is writ large over several important parts of this book. For Marxist theory and sustained revolutionary commitment, there has been indeed nothing else like *Monthly Review*. Its authentic Marxist analysis of developments across the globe, easily accessible yet sophisticated in the best sense of the word, its unwavering commitment to the cause of socialism and principled support to revolutionary struggles everywhere, have educated, encouraged and inspired socialists and radicals throughout the world. Paul Sweezy and Harry Magdoff have been a constant source of enlightenment and inspiration. For me personally, Paul Sweezy was and remains a model of what a Marxist intellectual should be in our times. In recent years I have much benefited from the wide-ranging work of Ellen Meiksins Wood and John Bellamy Foster's writings in the field of ecology.

The original impulse for this writing lay in my long-time interest in understanding why and how things had gone wrong with socialism in the Soviet Union. As the crisis in Soviet society deepened in the 1980s, the subject became a matter of still more serious concern. Sometime before 'the earthquake of 1989', in my Preface to Bertell Ollman's Indian publication, *Marxism: A Uncommon Introduction*, referring to Macpherson's view that 'the utility of Marxism as a means of understanding the world is increasing over time', I had added: '"the world" includes.... not only the advanced capitalist countries or India and the so-called Third World, but the world of "actually existing socialism" also, with its troublous past, continuing problems and the truly historical predicament today'. The predicament soon ended in the ignominious collapse of Soviet socialism and then of the Soviet Union itself. But no viable Marxist explanation of what had happened was forthcoming from within the country's communist movement – a situation that still persists; even the later, more informed or updated 'official' efforts are a string of eclectic propositions: 'serious mistakes'; 'wrong notions of the role of the Party and the state'; 'the failure to effect timely changes in the economy and its management'; the failure to 'deepen socialist democracy'; 'the erosion of ideological consciousness'; etc. In this situation, as the enemies' explanation – 'socialism has failed', 'Marxism is dead', etc. – held sway, there was a demand on me to share my understanding of what had happened. The opportunity to put my ideas together for the purpose came in the form of the invitation to deliver the Moin Shakir Memorial Lectures at the Marathwada University. As originally written or rather loosely expanded or updated in many places, these lectures – my 1991 response to the interrelated set of issues involved in the collapse of the Soviet Union – constitute the core of these notes, now being published as a book.

This response is obviously not an academic exercise, a work of scholarship or historical research, and it makes no claims, absolutely none, to originality. As the sub-title indicates, my response has a strong personal dimension to it. But this does not make it merely a declaration of faith. On the contrary, what is presented here is a serious argument in behalf of the continuing validity and relevance of socialism as a historically necessary, superior-to-capitalism, social order, and the need for the common people everywhere to struggle for it. Even as each chapter stands by itself, different chapters well hold together in support of this argument. The text apart, evidence in support of my argument is there, scattered all around us, only if we are willing to see; a little reason and ability to interconnect is all that is needed.

Not an academic exercise, these are notes of a militant in the movement, 'a small "C" communist', to borrow that most helpful self-description from E.P. Thompson. And the argument is addressed to fellow militants in what is left of the communist movement, to 'social democrats' who still remain socialist, to the new crop of radicals, in the social movements or outside them, struggling to find their bearings in a world now almost universally dominated by capitalism, and to all those on the Left who share my concern with the present and future of socialism. Even others may find it of interest for their present and future too is now involved in the present and future of socialism in a way that was never the case before. If anything, these notes are an exercise in theory, a plea to parties and activists on the Left for a return to the basics. Theory, it may be added, does not directly yield a political programme which is the task of political parties or activists on the ground. But it serves to provide a basic understanding of things, a perspective or sense of direction, most necessary for the success of any popular struggle. A struggling people will not get very far without some substantial knowledge of the structures they need to overthrow for their emancipation and a sense of direction in their struggle.

[The format of Notes has enabled me to deal with a wide range of issues in this regard, many of them raised with me by the concerned activists or friends on the Left. (The chapter on Marxism, for example, in its overall thrust and detail, is very much a response to an express request from two such friends, most eminent in the fields of literature and people's theatre in Punjab). The way the original lectures were planned and delivered, there is little direct reference to India, but relevance to India is more than implicit in the argument throughout these notes. The language (English), I know, is a handicap in reaching out to a larger readership, especially at the level of activists on the ground. I hope translation will help out as has already happened with some already published parts of these notes.]

I have already regretted the repetition that marks these notes and offered an explanation, not justification, for it; though even a justification is not to be entirely ruled out. Gunter Grass has said: 'In politics you have to repeat and repeat, like a parrot, ideas you know to be correct and proven as such, which is exhausting – you constantly hear the echo of your own voice, and end up sounding like a parrot even to yourself. But this is evidently part of the job, if one is to find any listeners at all in a world so full of different voices', or, I may add, when the noisy voice of those currently dominant in society seeks to drown all other voices and wants us to forget what was said earlier and has been proved to be true, or forbids what needs to be said or repeated anew today.

If my experience with the sophisticates of the academy or bourgeois ideology, or plain anti-socialist propagandists, is any guide, 'crudeness and simplification' is a charge sure to be brought against my argument. I will not here argue or complain over it, but borrow from Marcuse to suggest that, at times, crudeness and simplification also help to make the truth of an idea more visible. And truth of the socialist idea is my main concern in these notes.

During the heady, rebel days in the late sixties, students of Paris used to ask of everyone who would address them to first tell them: 'where do you speak from?' For every speaker, and for that matter every writer, inescapably speaks or writes from a particular philosophical-political standpoint and owes it to his audience or readers to publicly state it. It is only fair to acknowledge that I have written from the standpoint of Marxism, rather Marxism as I understand it. For I have no pretensions to scholarship in Marxism. I picked up some on the way and have found it useful not only in my politics or profession as a teacher but in living my life as well. This last is not just a formal statement. Knowing Marx does make a difference to what sense you make of life, how you understand, live and act in the world. 'Indeed, I must confess that Karl Marx made a man of me', is how George Bernard Shaw once put it. Marx, therefore, is important to me and, I believe, he is important to all of us, today more so than ever before, if for no other reason than this: the world we are living in is a capitalist world, more capitalist than ever before after the Soviet collapse, and Marx more than any other human being, then or now, devoted his life to explaining the reality of this world and his achievement here remains unrivalled. In one sense, this is what this book is about.

I know that the way I have been speaking or writing about Marx, about capitalism, socialism, and such other things, in recent years, not a few have thought of me as someone woefully out of sync with our post-modern, neo-liberal or globalised times, a 'dinosaur', as it were, from another age. Many will think the same of this book and will be similarly dismissive about its argument. This is nothing to be surprised at or complain about, only something that even the best among us have to endure. Paul Sweezy and Harry Magdoff had the distinction of being referred to as 'paleolithic sectarian survivals' in the aftermath of the Soviet collapse because they continued to argue and speak up for socialism. Recently we have had the example of the Nobel Laureate Gunter Grass and the world famous sociologist Pierre Bourdieu. Holding that neoliberalism is 'simply a return to the methods of nineteenth-century Manchester liberalism', 'a strange revolution that restores the past but presents itself as progressive, transforming regression itself into a form of progress', they have said: 'It does this so well that those who oppose it are made to appear regressive themselves. This is something we have both endured: we are readily treated as old-fashioned, "has-beens", "throwbacks"... "dinosaurs".' Grass and Bourdieu have nevertheless insisted that one must continue to speak up.

So have Paul Sweezy and Harry Magdoff, all along. Some years back, apropos post-Soviet capitalist triumphalism, they had written: 'Capitalism's victory settles nothing. In its global form, it encompasses ever more people and intensifies their exploitation and oppression. History shows that there have been alternatives in the past, and reason tells us that there will be others in the future.... It is of the greatest importance to keep the radical tradition alive and vigorous, ready to undergrid and give direction to the revolutionary struggles that lie ahead'. This is how I too had conceived this writing in 1991. Since then, the euphoria over 'capitalism's victory' long over, the struggles that lay ahead are already on the agenda of the peoples everywhere. This is where I locate whatever relevance this book has.

I would like to thank the Institute for Development and Communication, Chandigarh and its Director Dr. Pramod Kumar, for providing the facilities to complete and put together the manuscript of this book and getting the book itself into shape for the printer and publisher at Delhi. I can never be too thankful to Ashwini Kumar for the hard work he personally put into all this. I am grateful to my wife, Mohinder Kaur, for bearing with me as I struggled with this writing in Delhi, Shimla and Chandigarh. Not exactly thanks but something more is due to Priyaleen, Shimareet, Meenakshi Gopinath and Bertell Ollman who, each in her or his own way, sustained me in writing these notes. The responsibility for the argument, of course, remains mine.

Randhir Singh

March 2004

Ecological Crisis and Future of Socialism

The destructive consequences inherent in the structural logic of capitalism are today all the more manifest, now that capitalism is living beyond what in any rational understanding of historical processes should have been its legitimate life span. Its positive potential almost exhausted, certainly far outbalanced by its negative outcome, these consequences are today obviously visible in the economy, politics, life and culture of the countries of advanced capitalism and even more of the periphery of the global capitalist system. But there is one consequence which may well turn out to be ultimately disastrous for humankind as a whole and this is the threat capitalism has come to pose to the natural environment, to the ecology of our planet as the habitat of the human species.

In the aftermath of the explosion of the first atom bombs over Hiroshima and Nagasaki in August 1944 – incidentally, not the last or closing act of the Second World War as it was claimed to be, but, as Prof. PMS Blackett has pointed out, the opening act of America's Cold War against the Soviet Union – and the quick acquisition of nuclear weapons by the Soviet Union, there was widespread fear that a nuclear war could terminate the whole human enterprise on this earth. There was persistent speculation about ghastly radio-active poisoning and nuclear winter over the entire globe. Peaceful co-existence, guaranteed by 'mutual armed deterrence' followed, but the threat of a nuclear war remained. With the defeat of the Soviet Union in the Cold War and its subsequent departure from the historical scene, the nuclear threat may have receded somewhat but has not disappeared. It remains very much a part of the global politics of the dominant capitalist powers, and not only of these powers. For even as the U.S. persists with its Nuclear Missile Defence or Falcon programmes, proliferation of nuclear weapons has continued, bringing even some minor players into the game. But even if the nuclear politics of global capitalism manages to avoid a holocaust ending of the world – which can never be discounted – it is by no means certain that the essential conditions for the survival and development of civilised society as we know it or can think of will continue to exist. For a new threat to the human habitat on this earth, within a thinkable time span, has emerged and this encompasses a variety of ecological processes and trends, known and studied for more than a hundred years, which have now cumulatively resulted in what has generally come to be recognised as *the environmental crisis* of our times which is deepening and gathering momentum with every passing decade, if not year.

II

The major elements of this crisis, which is a truly global phenomenon, are now well known and require no elaboration here: rapid depletion of natural resources (renewable and non-renewable) and general pollution of earth's resources in land, water and air; the greenhouse effect stemming from the massive combustion of fossil fuels, combined with the accelerating destruction of carbon dioxide-absorbing tropical forests; acidification, so that there is acid rain which destroys lakes and forests and other forms of vegetation; desertification, so that there is worldwide destruction of wilderness, denuding and decimation of forests; the weakening of the ozone layer in the upper atmosphere that protects human beings and other forms of life from the sun's potentially deadly ultraviolet rays, with epidemic rise in skin cancer in parts of the world; the erosion and destruction of top soils and expansion of deserts by predatory agricultural methods; the spread of radio-active isotopes and proliferation of all sorts of highly toxic chemicals and hazardous wastes; pollution of rivers and lakes, depletion of ground water and fouling of land and surface waters through industrial dumping and excessive use of chemical fertilisers and pesticides – as soils become leached and as the very bedrock becomes contaminated with unaccountable and accumulated nuclear and toxic wastes, the waters are building up unmanageable levels of dangerous chemicals; other potentially dangerous consequences of man-made changes in climate (global warming, etc.); extinction of myriad species and the dying out of gene pools and marine life at an accelerating pace; mounting pollution of even the oceans, once thought to be an infinite repository of all kinds of wastes but now, in what has become one of the most visible aspects of environmental crisis, seen to be fragile and vulnerable like all the rest of nature.....

Earth's health status is now indeed most precarious and any number of well-researched studies are regularly documenting and reporting on it. The Washington-based Worldwatch Institute, for example, has been, year after year, reporting about the disappearing forest cover, ravaged grasslands, declining per capita food production, polluted air and water and a hundred other symptoms of environmental degradation that is taking place. As a recent report has it: protecting ozone shield in heavily-populated latitudes of the northern hemisphere is thinning twice as fast as scientists thought just a few years ago – this means an estimated additional 200,000 skin cancer fatalities in the US alone in the next 50 years and a million more lives worldwide; a minimum of 140 plant and animal species are condemned to extinction each day by the destruction of their tropical rain forest habitat; atmospheric levels of heat-trapping carbon dioxide (emitted from fossil fuel burning in automobiles and power plants) are now 26 per cent higher than the pre-industrial concentration, and continue to increase; the earth's surface was warmer in 1990 than in any year since record keeping began in the mid-19th century – six of the seven warmest years on record have occurred since 1980; the earth is losing 25 billion tonnes of top soil every year and forests are vanishing at the rate of some 17 million hectares per year; and so on. The situation, as reported by the Institute, is worsening with every passing year.

A distinguished team of scientists writing in *Science* magazine have recently stated: 'The rates, scale, kinds, and combinations of changes occurring now are fundamentally different from those at any other time in history; we are changing the Earth more rapidly than we are understanding it'. A most serious consequence of the way we are 'changing the Earth' is the environmental or ecological crisis we are now facing. With somewhere between a third and a half of the land surface of the earth now transformed by human action, the carbon dioxide content of the atmosphere, as more recently reported, has increased by some 30 per cent since the Industrial Revolution. The rates of species extinction are now 100 to 1000 times those prior to the human domination of the earth. Over-cutting has already decimated ecosystems in Canada, Brazil, Malaysia. Worldwide, across continents, tropical rainforests, our 'green lungs', are being felled at the rate of nearly 55,000 square miles a year. At that rate, according to the Harvard ecologist Edward O. Wilson, the world's rain forests will be reduced by half in thirty years, and some 10–22 per cent of rain forest species will be doomed in the next three decades. And this is to say nothing of the thousands upon thousands of species of birds, amphibians, turtles, bats, primates, cetaceans, the hundreds of thousands of invertebrates, and the untold numbers of plant species that have already been driven to extinction over the last two centuries or so. Species extinction has accelerated to such a rate that, according to Wilson, some 50,000 species a year, or about six every hour, are being doomed to eventual extinction – 'a genuine holocaust'... Ecologist Jared Diamond of UCLA concludes that if current trends continue, even taking into account all the uncertainties, 'something like half the species that now exist will go extinct or will be on the verge of going extinct in the next century'. According to the environmentalist group Greenpeace, at the current rate of destruction, the Amazon, which represents a quarter of the planet's forests and is one of its most diverse reserves of plants and animals could disappear, reduced to scattered clumps of trees, within the next 50 years. It reports: 'Over four and a half centuries, from 1500 to around 1970, only one per cent of the rainforest was destroyed. In the three decades since, 590,000 square metres of forests have been chopped down. That's 15 per cent of the Amazon – an area bigger than France'. Mining and smelting have ruined whole mountains, valleys and rivers from Arizona to Chile, from Brazil to New Guinea. Oil extraction has decimated land and water from Alaska to the North Sea. Petrochemical biocides are ruining soil from the U.S. to Uzbekistan. Entire ecosystems like coral reefs, mountain areas, dry tropical rainforests and other tropical habitats that evolved over millions of years are now being destroyed in a biohistorical blink of an eye. So far, an estimated 27 per cent of the world's coral reefs have been either destroyed or damaged by human activity and the rest are endangered. Recent scientific reports have suggested that global warming trends are much greater than previously thought. According to the United Nations Intergovernmental Panel on Climate Change (IPCC), the main official scientific body studying global warming, the earth's climate has been relatively stable over the ten thousand years since the last ice age, with global temperature changes of less than one degree centigrade per century during this entire period. In comparison, current climate change scenarios now project an increase in global mean surface temperature of 1.5 to 6 degrees centigrade by 2100. According to a study across four continents, claimed to be most comprehensive so far and published in the magazine *Nature*, climate change over the next fifty years is expected to drive a quarter of land animals and plants into extinction. More than 1 million species will be lost by 2050, and much of the loss so far – more than one in 10 of all plants and animals – is already irreversible because of the extra global warming gases already discharged into the atmosphere. Among the other catastrophic problems that may ensue as a result of current warming scenarios are rising sea levels (projected to rise fifteen to ninety-five centimetres by 2100). Mountains glaciers are melting worldwide as is Sea Ice in both the Arctic and Antarctic. Already, Venice is being written of as virtually a ghost city, with only those residents remaining who are involved in the travel and trade industry. Low-lying areas like Bangladesh, the Maldives, South East Asia and the Pacific Islands are believed to be most vulnerable to rising sea levels. There is rapidly increasing desertification in arid and semi-arid regions, declining agricultural productivity (especially in tropical and semitropical regions). The Sahara is expanding into all countries that bordered it. China and Central Asian countries like Kazakhstan are faced with topsoil loss and erosion on a scale not easily imagined; half of Kazakhstan's huge grasslands are gone, it appears, for ever. According to a recent article in the journal *Science*, US scientists predict an imminent emergence of various threats – outbreaks of malaria, disease-stricken corals, fungus-infested trees and parasite infestations among insects. Human health is deteriorating everywhere. Country after country is reporting a loss of sustainability. *Running on Empty*, a report recently released by British-based development agency Tearfund says that two out of three people in the world will face water shortages by 2025 and we will increasingly witness 'a new phenomenon – "water refugees" – millions of people being forced to leave their home in search of clean water'. Some years back, the eminent scientist, late Carl Sagan had warned of a future of nations going to war over water.

While most damage to the environment has been done by the 'developed' countries of the first world, America leading, the so-called 'developing' countries of the third world are not lagging behind. Industrial air and water pollution, and toxic waste generated by Asian industry, for example, is increasing at several times the rate of GNP growth. It has been calculated and reported that although Asia's emissions of greenhouse and other gases are still small in per capita terms, in absolute terms Asia will exceed Europe and then US combined in sulphur dioxide emissions by the year 2005. Asia's carbon dioxide emissions are likely to surpass that of all industrialised countries by 2015. Along with excessive deforestation, Asia is suffering a tragic loss of biodiversity. Nearly three-quarters of the natural habitat in Asia has been lost or irreversibly degraded, and it is estimated that Asia will lose a higher proportion of its species and natural ecosystems than any other region during the next twenty-five years. We have the World Bank's warning that Asia's environmental problems 'are approaching thresholds of unacceptably high social and economic costs including increasing health costs and mortality, reduced output in resource-based sectors, and irreversible loss of biodiversity and overall environmental quality'.

It is really impossible to compute the ongoing ecological devastation in the world and its short and long-run consequences for humankind. What has been stated above, far from complete, actually does no more than hint at the extent of the environmental crisis, the far reaching and often subtle interconnections of its various components and some of its more obvious consequences. But it is enough to indicate the general nature of the crisis as a radical, and growing, disjunction between on the one hand the demands placed on the environment by the modern global economy, and on the other the capacity of the natural forces embedded in the environment to meet these demands. There is 'the brutal fact' that the normal course of social production inexorably destroys the *natural* basis of society. Until as recently as the 1960s, nature was able to buffer the effects of production, even act as a 'sink' tank to absorb the pollution it produced. Now this function is breaking down in a proliferating and incalculable way across multiple ecosystems. There is not only a global crisis of resource exhaustion, the biosphere, the human habitat itself, is getting damaged almost beyond repair. Against the nature we used to have – regular and dependable, self-perpetuating and friendly, beautiful as well as life-sustaining – we have created an artificial nature – unstable and unpredictable, market-manipulated and hostile, ugly as well as life-denying – which is making living, even breathing on this earth increasingly impossible. As the authors of an article in a recent issue of the magazine *Natural History* put it: 'The throwaway society that has emerged during the late twentieth century uses so much energy, emits so much carbon, and generates so much air pollution, toxic waste, and rubbish that it is strangling itself.'

III

Awareness of the environmental crisis has grown rapidly in recent decades, particularly sharply after 1972 when the Club of Rome (an informal association of corporate leaders, researchers and government officials) published its *The Limits of Growth*, and posed the issue as the very survival of the planet. Concern over the crisis has produced volumes upon volumes of data on the extent of damage being caused to the global environment, much scientific comment and philosophising on the issue and a certain ascendancy of 'the green fashion' the world over – what with endless flurry of activity over commissions and conferences on environment, Days and Sumitts dedicated to the Earth (as to its Water, Ozone Layer, Forests, etc.) wherein ministers, politicians and officials, national and international, taking time off ceremonial tree planting, make trans-Atlantic and trans-Pacific flights, with NGOs in tow or opposition, to talk about Ozone layer depletion, global warming, 'greenhouse effect', tropical deforestation, and so on, everyone flaunting a 'greener than thou' attitude. Governments regularly proclaim their concern for the environment as do the international agencies that keep coming up to serve the noble cause. Even Gorbachev has got on to one – the Geneva-based *Green Cross International* – to pontificate about the new century as 'the century of the environment'. Corporations too have not lagged behind. Today there is hardly an ad which doesn't exhort you to 'save the environment', to put an end to pollution and poisoning of earth's air and water.

Dire warnings have been issued about the impending catastrophe and there is no end to the suggestions made to avert it. We have been advised to overcome prejudice, greed and lethargy, and the comfortable notion that things can't be all that urgent because mankind has been facing similar problems for a long time; to treat bio-diversity with respect; to encourage the use of natural and recyclable materials, save energy and minimise wastage; to shift from fossil fuels (coal and petroleum) to renewable sources of energy derived from the sun and the wind; to plant trees and avoid the use of throw-away beverage containers; to redesign our cities and transportation networks; to lessen automobile use and introduce the bicycle as the main mode of transport; to show personal restraint with regard to the growth of both production and consumption; to 'Save Our Skies – Be Ozone Friendly', etc. etc. There are suggestions 'to get out of this mess by marrying traditional knowledge with modern science and technology'. A whole new academic discipline, 'Ecological Economics', has come up and 'ecological pricing' – putting ecological costs into price of commodities – is advocated. Pontificates Oystein Dahle, a retired vice-president of the Norwegian branch of the Exxon oil company: 'Socialism collapsed because it did not allow prices to tell the economic truth. Capitalism may collapse because it does not allow prices to tell the ecological truth'. An Al Gore declares that 'rescue of the environment' must become 'the central organising principle for civilisation', confronting 'nothing less than the current logic of world civilisation'. Others have argued, with details, for an entirely new 'ecological *Weltanschauung* to found an ethic adequate to our present crisis'. Typical of the more comprehensive measures suggested is Brundtland Commission's Tokyo Declaration (1987) to 'all the nations of the world, both jointly and individually', calling upon them 'to integrate sustainable development into their goals and to adopt the following principles to guide their actions' – which principles were then listed as: (1) renew growth, (2) change the quality of growth, (3) conserve and enhance the resource base, (4) insure a sustainable level of population, (5) reorient technology and manage risks, (6) integrate environment and economics in decision-making, (7) reform international economic relations, and (8) strengthen international cooperation.

Such advice, suggestions and principles have flowed in an endless stream from concerned environmentalists, scholarly tomes and reports, and commissions, conferences and summits over the past three decades – but to remain, overwhelmingly, only so many platitudes or pious intentions. More and more environment-related agreements and commissions are coming up with more and more funds – like the Global Environment Facility (GEF) to be handled by the World Bank – but very little happens on the ground. Because environment is a visibly big thing in the affluent west and makes for a certain legitimacy everywhere, lots of money has been let loose by U.N. bodies and donor agencies, by international NGOs, many of them flush with funds which they do not know how to use, and even by governments and ministries in large parts of the third world, but the results have been mostly of symbolic value. Even as there is a near-universal acknowledgement of the ecological problems, most solutions remain facile. Many concerned citizens argue and act as if concluding international agreements or making more proclamations, recycling and using earth-friendly products, or practising self-vigilance and restraints constitute a fundamental solution to the current environmental crisis. In other words, while it is realised that if there is any single problem that we have to face and overcome today, it is the problem of making our economic peace with the demands of the environment so that 'the vital processes of material provisioning do not contaminate the green-blue film on which life itself depends', and while the warnings in this regard are daily becoming louder and clearer, it is equally a fact that no substantive action has materialised so far. The Agenda 21 of the high profile Rio Earth Summit (the United Nations Conference on Environment and Development, 1992) remains essentially unimplemented. The Johannesburg Summit, a decade later was, if anything, a journey backward. 'Rio + 10 = Johannesburg = 0' – this is how a leading Indian newspaper editorially summed up. As Lester Brown of the World Watch Institute once lamented, even as the governments have been setting up national environmental protection agencies, the degradation of the environment continues. We have Carl Sagan's poignant question: 'Who speaks for the human species? Who speaks for Earth?'

IV

There is the increasing recognition that it is the unsustainable system of economic development in the affluent countries of the North which is primarily responsible for the current environmental crisis. The rampant consumerism of recent decades has only deepened this crisis even as, with its rock music gadgetry, fast foods and Coca Cola, it has forged a new, parallel and temporary – that is , as long as youth lasts – society and created what the African historian Joseph Kizerbo, calls 'homo coca-colens' as a distinct part of what has come to be described as 'the American way of life'. The affluence of the North – even its consumerism and the 'American way of life' – is envied, admired and desired almost everywhere, not the least in the countries of the poor South. The realisation however is growing that the North's system of production and consumption cannot be maintained even in the North, let alone exported to the South. The World Watch Institute has been urging these countries to face the sheer unsustainability of their own current pattern of consumption. In their persistence with it, the North is even seen to be possessed by a death wish: it is eager to 'sell the rope with which it is to hang', as a critic has put it. Others, alarmed by the possibility of the Chinese and the rest entering the consumer age have warned that three planets Earth would be necessary for the whole of the world population to reach North American consumption levels. The general adoption of North's unsustainable system of economic development – enormously damaging already – would make the whole system instantly collapse. At present the U.S. population, less than 5 per cent of the world population, consumes 25 per cent of total available energy resources. We can well imagine what would happen if the 95 per cent adopted the same consumption pattern, trying to squeeze *their* 25 per cent out of the remaining 75 per cent.

It has been therefore argued that no meaningful reversal of current trends can take place unless the rich countries of the world learn to make do with much less of everything and help the poor countries of the world to improve their living standards. What we have, however, is no effort at self restraint on the part of the rich countries, only advice to the poor ones not to pollute the world with their economic development. Even when there is agreement, at summits and elsewhere, that, responsible as they are for the environmental mess in the world, the rich countries must share the burden of cleaning it up by assisting the poor countries, financially and otherwise, to shift to a more sustainable mode of development, there is near-absolute reluctance to do so. Promises are made but never kept. Instead, policies of globalisation and economic liberalisation are imposed on these poor countries generating competitive pressure for them to plunder their forests, fisheries, and other natural resources to increase export earnings, and to adopt minimal environmental standards so as to attract foreign investors – all the while reproducing, along with the unsustainable pattern of economic development, their own parallel societies of mindless consumerism and 'homo coca-colens' in the affluent enclaves at the top.

I will be returning to some of these issues later as part of my discussion of the overall inadequacy, lack of vision and the politics of the mainstream response to the growing ecological crisis. Immediately, I would like to make a brief reference to three somewhat specific issues involved in this response – population growth, environmental NGOs and the notion of 'sustainable development'.

Quite often, the cause of current environmental crisis is traced easily to *too many people* – and the overriding concern here is with population growth in the South, where it is also seen as the cause of its endemic poverty. Adopting the neo-Malthusian framework of 'carrying capacity', it is argued that population is outgrowing our limited natural resources, and therefore the long run solution to the environmental problem is to limit population growth. Certainly, world population, which is growing by 92 million annually, of which 88 million are being added in the so-called developing countries, is an important factor in the situation, and the importance of rational population stabilisation policies to curb this growth rate, especially in the South, is not to be denied. But serious scholarly work in this area has convincingly established that concurrence of rapid population growth and environmental degradation does not necessarily reflect a direct causal connection between them. Population, as just mentioned, is certainly a factor in the situation, but as Barry Commoner, the eminent scientist, has argued, environmental quality is largely governed, not by population growth, but by the nature of the technologies of production. And the important fact to be recognised here is that the existing mode of production, in its pursuit of profit, does not care what damage its way of utilisation of natural resources, its technologies of production, inflict upon the environment. Focussing on population, more specifically on population growth in the South only serves to obscure the environment-destroying implications, indeed the ecological non-viability of the existing production system of the North.

This apart, insofar as population is a factor in the relentless destruction of the biosphere that is on, and population control remains on the agenda of environmental action, the causal connection between population growth and poverty needs to be properly understood. It is now a well-established fact that it is poverty that causes excessive population growth, rather than the other way around. And as Marxists have repeatedly pointed out, it is a *structurally* important aspect, indeed the basic contradiction of capitalism, that it continuously produces and reproduces poverty within societies and even more on a global scale, which has at the end of it all resulted in the impoverishment of an overwhelming majority of humankind today. The implications are obvious. Barry Commoner, discussing the historical, capitalist roots of the environmental crisis, has written: 'My own purely personal conclusion is not scientific but political: the world population crisis, which is the ultimate outcome of the exploitation of poor nations by rich ones, ought to be remedied by returning to the poor countries enough of the wealth taken from them to give their peoples both the reason and the resources voluntarily to limit their own fertility.... if the root cause of the world population crisis is poverty, then to end it we must abolish poverty. And if the cause of poverty is the grossly unequal distribution of the world's wealth, then to end poverty, and with it the population crisis, we must redistribute that wealth, among nations and within them.'

No long-run solution of the problems of poverty, population and environmental crisis can afford to ignore this vital truth.

As in several other areas of social action, there has been a very impressive growth in voluntary environmental activism the world over in recent years, often with the backing of United Nations, international financial institutions like the World Bank and even multinational corporations. The third world too has shared in the contemporary efflorescence of related Non-Governmental Organisations (NGOs), much of it with government support and massive foreign funding. The early enthusiastic participation of people, particularly the young, in the growing number of environment protection groups or NGOs even persuaded some to see in this environmental activism a movement with a radical potential. This potential however, if it is at all there, has remained unrealised. Understanding of wider issues of economy and politics have been generally lacking. Even at its best, the projects of these groups or organisations have remained largely localised and without any genuine national impact. At its worst environment has also become a pastime, a leisure-time activity; there are a whole lot of young people in this so-called 'movement', landing an easy job in one NGO or another and living a relatively easy life. Any number of NGOs have been either co-opted by governments or otherwise contained and rendered impotent by the dominant commercial ethic of our market societies. With more and more people being professionally enticed, not a few of NGOs have degenerated into bureaucratised, careerist set-ups. Many NGOs in the South act as virtual clones of northern environmental NGOs from which they receive their funds.

Funding, foreign or otherwise, remains a serious problem for the NGOs. Financial dependence it involves reduces efforts to attain self-reliance and habituates the recipients to cater to the particular interests of the funding agency. Concern for the funder also constrains an NGO from involving itself and its clientele in issues that view environmental problems from a broader economic or political perspective. The United Nations Conference on Environment and Development at Rio de Janeiro in Brazil in 1992, popularly known as the 'Earth Summit' – arguably the most important event in the environment movement so far, 'the ultimate in movement conferencing, in fact the ultimate in all conferencing' as it has been described – revealed not only how well the movement had become increasingly dependent on not just 'foreign funding' but big money houses, but also got corrupted by this dependence. Several of the NGOs present there were seen, and came to be described, as 'the wolves in sheep's clothing' – business NGOs with green veneer, representing all of the most scandal-ridden industrial sectors like mining, agro-chemicals, pharmaceuticals, oil, power generation and forestry. This is not to deny the still significant presence and role of independent or militant NGOs in the environmental movement. But even here, as scholars like Bennis have pointed out, 1992 Earth Summit on, the United States has systematically attempted to co-opt and thwart the militant NGOs, to replace their legitimate political demands with its own corporate and imperial line – and not without success always.

Therefore, while the work of best of them is indeed deserving of admiration, it is a mistake to look for answers to the environmental crisis, as not a few have done, in the local initiatives of voluntary activism of the NGOs. Taking into account such serious issues as sources of funding, vulnerability to manipulation by vested interests, coverage and development of initiatives and innovations, record of overall achievement so far, and the limitations inherent in local initiatives where basic issues of economy or politics are involved, there is little to share optimism about the effectiveness of NGOs in reversing the current trends and protecting the environment. A 'romantic' NGO approach to the environmental crisis is only a convenient way out of confronting the basic issues involved – an evasion really, which has found a characteristic expression in the fashionable slogan: 'think globally and act locally'.

The gravity of the ecological crisis has evoked, along with powerful denunciations of the exponential growth of consumerism, hyperbolic declarations in behalf of 'an environmental revolution', or the 'first Global Revolution', 'a complete restructuring of the international economic system', which is deemed imperative now. Governments, policy makers, corporate planners, and even individuals have been called upon to 'restructure global economy, dramatically change human reproductive behaviour and alter values and life-styles' to save earth from destruction. Somewhat more specifically, the causes underlying the current ecological crisis have been located in 'the extraordinary triumphs of science and productive technology' which are now making our planet uninhabitable, or in 'economic growth' or, more perceptively, 'pattern of economic development' which, seen to be inevitably at odds with the demands of the environment, has brought us to the brink of an ecological disaster. The present growth trends, it is argued, cannot be sustained for long and therefore we must turn to a pattern of growth or development which is sustainable.

'Sustainable development' has been the buzzword in the international environmental lobby as well as national policies on environment since the early 1990s. Ever since the Brundtland Report (1987) injected this word into political environmental discourse, it has been used by everyone from the World Bank to Greenpeace. All now give at least lip service to the goal of a 'sustainable development' which preserves and protects the global biosphere. The concept has caught on, although its meaning remains elusive. As an approach to economic development, it does not articulate any well-defined strategy for action. Rather, ill-defined and vague, it is amenable to interpretation according to one's inclinations. Which perhaps explains its magic spread and wide acceptability. Pointing out that '"sustainable development" means different things to different people', British environmentalist, Radcliff, has written: 'its very strength is its vagueness.'

Vagueness of the concept notwithstanding, the context and general drift of its use points, beyond a needful aspiration, to a substantial assumption underlying it as an ecological project. In this, its meaningful sense, sustainable development assumes not only that development is essential to the elimination of poverty and provision of decent living for all human beings, but that it has to be a development which meets human needs without destroying the natural systems; which can continue indefinitely into the human future without generating such constraints as resource depletion, environmental injury, burgeoning human population or economic and political repression; which would address the urgent problems of present generations without penalising future generations. This is indeed what a rational and humane economic development should be. Needless to add, however, that despite all the noise being made about it, such sustainable development is *not* proceeding anywhere in the world today (except, perhaps, a pioneering effort in Cuba). Meanwhile the environment continues to be ravaged by the modern global economy.

It is interesting and to be noted that the concept of sustainable development has emerged from those countries whose 'pattern of development' is now seen to be unsustainable for long. This obviously suggests that any action on sustainable development can be initiated only with an understanding of the existing pattern of development in these countries and the unsustainable demand it makes on our planet's natural resources. Yet the conventional debate on sustainable development is marked by a remarkable lack of interest in understanding the existing pattern or an equally remarkable inability to understand it. Even when it is realised that 'the market is ill-adapted to deal with long-term effects, inter-generational responsibilities and common property resources', the government is expected and urged to discipline and control it, ignoring the fact that under the existing (capitalist) pattern of development, it is the market which controls the government and not the other way around, that the solution thus preferred is itself a problem. If any new proof of it was needed, the Earth Summit at Rio and international conferencing on environment since then have convincingly demonstrated how the market, that is, the dominant economic interests, can overrun all the policy pronouncements and platitudes mouthed by government leaders about global solidarity to deal with the problems of environment and development on the global scale. The advocates of the much-needed 'global revolution' have not themselves failed to confess that inspite of dire warnings sounded so often in the past, the requisite political will has not been forthcoming, few if any government has the courage to face the problems that any meaningful move towards a 'sustainable development' involves.

World's growing ecological consciousness still fails to recognise that the 'pattern of development' it sees as the danger to the future of the planet has a name, capitalism – a system of production whose structural imperatives necessarily degrade the environment. It is nonsense to talk about 'sustainable development', unless it means a break with these imperatives, that is, a reordering of our socio-economic system in such a way that production decisions are based on needs that are prior to production, rather than basing needs on production decisions.

V

As suggested above, what is most glaringly missing in the conventional response to the current ecological crisis is a realistic analysis of the present system of economic development, of the forces inherent in it that are almost inexorably propelling it on to degrade and destroy environment and prevent effective action being taken to counter the threats to global survival. Such analysis could also serve to provide some real basis and concrete content to the concept of 'sustainable development'. Perhaps Marx could still be of some help here in understanding and therefore averting the impending ecological disaster. Maybe in these 'anti-Marx times', we could still profitably turn or return to him, above all to his analysis of what the environmentalist critics invariably refer to as 'a pattern of unsustainable economic development' but which till recently had a proper name, capitalism – a name which, capitalism having become so pervasively powerful as to be invisible, has virtually disappeared from today's economic and political discourse.

In this connection, it may be pointed out that our environmental awareness is typically a product of the period of capitalist development. In pre-capitalist society, an explicit notion of environmental limits was generally lacking. For not only were those limits not yet reached, but ecological 'insights' which nowadays seem to require extensive research were at that time matters of common knowledge born of long experience (for example, the advantages of crop rotation and composting in agriculture). Present-day environmental 'consciousness' arose only after not only were nature's limits breached but those earlier, environmentally benign approaches had been destroyed by the routine functioning of the capitalist market economy (in which, for example, commercial agriculture gravitates towards large-scale mono-culture). Environmental consciousness has grown with the growth of the environmental crisis. Even in a world of all-pervasive capitalism, it should not require much historical imagination to recognise that the roots of this crisis lie in capitalism as it has developed in the last three or four centuries.

It is not that ecological crises were entirely unknown in earlier, pre-capitalist societies. All human communities must live in and off their environment, in contradiction or strained relation as it were with nature. In their interaction with nature, to secure the conditions of their own survival and reproduction, human beings never leave the environment untouched and unchanged, and many human practices throughout history have been categorically destructive. Even the earlier pre-capitalist societies are thus known to have been vulnerable to regional environmental degradation, often as a result of human interventions to extract a larger surplus product than sustainable. We have the examples of Roman and Mayan civilisations, apart from the conspicuous case of the Sumerian civilisation, one of the most advanced civilisations during its time, which was virtually wiped out when land degradation proceeded too far. Even in the post-Roman feudal Europe, depletion of soil and over grazing were partly responsible for recurrent famines which in turn led to epidemics. But, rare and regional, such ecological crises never threatened a wholesale disaster for humankind. The traditional, pre-capitalist era communities always recognised the need to protect environment and treated nature with respect, even reverence. They not only put a value on living in harmony with nature, the technologies their economies involved allowed nature to recoup and recover itself for life's production and reproduction processes to go on. Besides, right from the hunter-gatherer stage of human history, communities have paid attention not only to production but also to the reproduction of the conditions of production. Anthropologists have studied conservation practices in hunting by primitive tribes – like not hunting during the mating and the calving season, marking areas of a hunt and not returning to them for a specific duration of time, etc. Similarly in agriculture – seed collection, varietal improvement of seeds over successive generations through experimentation and conscious propagation, periodic fallowing of land to regenerate soil fertility, etc. have been age-old practices.

The advent of capitalism meant a radical change in the situation. On the one hand there was not only a shift from natural resource-based activities like agriculture to industry on a large scale, both agricultural and industrial production – as in the agricultural and industrial revolutions of the 17th and 18th centuries – came to be geared to the market. On the other hand, methods of production yielding maximum profits for the capitalist took precedence over any concern for the environment. Capitalism is an economic system that is driven by insatiable hunger for profits and capital accumulation regardless of the consequences for human beings or nature in the present or the future. The result was a qualitatively new phase in the degradation and destruction of the environment.

This was evident in the criticism the ecological effects of the new economic system attracted even as it came up in England. Any number of sensitive contemporaries – poets, novelists, journalists, physicians, romantic social analysts and defenders of the working class – have left behind eloquent testimony to the horrors of the new industrial system. England's Midlands came to be called a 'Black Country' because so much of the vegetation had been destroyed. Not only nature but human beings, particularly factory workers, too were ravaged. Engels, giving a graphic account of their living conditions, was particularly concerned with environmental toxins, overcrowding, bad sanitation and inadequate ventilation. Marx too noted it and analysing it all later, pointed out that capitalism, a system driven by market imperatives and the commodification of all social life has a historically unique and systemic tendency to wasteful production and ecological degradation.

Today, capitalism having become a truly dominant global system, its tendency to ecological degradation has assumed proportions so alarming that for the first time in human history, we seem capable of 'ecocide', that is, destroying the entire ecological community altogether. Hence, not only the heightened environmental awareness as a product of the period of late capitalist development, but, also the basic point I am wanting to make, namely, the failure of the effort so far to stem the environmental degradation which is traceable to its basic limitation: a failure to recognise and strike at the core of the problem which lies in the structural logic of capitalism as a mode of production.

This, let me emphasise, is not to indulge in any economic reductionism or determinism, to establish a simple cause and effect relationship for all ecological problems or to oversimplify the vast and complex issues of the contemporary environmental crisis. It absolutely does not obviate the need for methodical investigation of reality, precise analysis of the autonomous existence of every major or minor threat to environment – here as anywhere else concrete analysis of a concrete situation remains basic to any kind of effective political praxis, of human intervention here and now. This can never be overemphasised, for not unoften Marxian theory in its ideological deformation has tended to rest content with abstract or 'grand' theorising, with servile and stereotyped, essentially irrefutable and therefore meaningless propositions, which have included blaming capitalism in general for every conceivable evil on earth. Such propositions, born of what I have elsewhere described as *holistic* error in Marxian analysis, are a barrier to understanding concrete reality; empty of meaning and devoid of results, they are impotent politically, just as abstract references to socialism or the need for revolution have often become empty formulas, the ideological mask of passivity. But, in turn, we must not commit the opposite *empiricistic* error – dominant in mainstream social thinking and social science – and fail to see the threats to environment in their vital interconnections with *the whole* that is the capitalist mode of production whose structural thrust historically has always been, and today more so than ever before, *against* environment, making an ecological catastrophe impossible to avoid within the capitalist system.

Even the conventional environmentalism is , more or less vaguely, aware of these interconnections, when it speaks of 'unsustainable pattern of economic development', 'the burden of economic growth on environment', 'the environmental havoc wrought by industrialism', etc. But it fails to see the historical specificity of this 'pattern of economic development', 'economic growth', or 'industrialism', perceiving it only as a matter of economic production or development in general. Marx had long ago pointed out: 'When we speak of production, we always have in mind production at a definite stage of social development.... in order to speak of production at all, we must either trace the historical process of development in its various phases, or declare at the very beginning that we are dealing with one particular historical epoch, for instance with modern bourgeois production.... The determinations which apply to production in general must rather be set apart in order not to allow the unity which stems from the very fact that the subject, mankind, and the object, nature, are the same, to obscure the essential difference.' This essential difference is precisely what conventional environmentalism fails to recognise.

Ted Benton has rightly pointed out: 'What is required is the recognition that each form of social/economic life has its own specific mode and dynamic of interrelation with its own specific contextual conditions, resource materials, energy sources and naturally mediated unintended consequences (forms of 'waste', 'pollution', etc.) The ecological problems of any form of social and economic life... have to be theorised as the outcome of the specific structure of natural/social articulation.' Apropos this, underlining the historical specificity of capitalism, Marx had written that under the capitalist production, 'for the first time, nature becomes purely an object for men, nothing more than a matter of utility. It ceases to be acknowledged as a power for itself, and even the theoretical cognition of its autonomous laws appears merely as a ruse for its subjection to human needs, whether as object of consumption or as means of production. It is this same tendency which makes capital drive beyond national boundaries and prejudices, and equally beyond nature worship.... Capitalism is destructive towards, and constantly revolutionises, all this, tearing down all barriers which impede the development of the productive forces, the extension of the range of needs, the differentiation of production, and the exploitation and exchange of all natural and spiritual powers.'

Pointing out a fundamental contradiction between the *ecosphere*, or 'natural environment,' and the *technosphere*, the human-created system of production and distribution, Barry Commoner has written: 'What we call the "environmental crisis" – the array of critical unsolved problems ranging from local toxic dumps to the disruption of global climate – is a product of the drastic mismatch between the cyclical, conservative, and self-consistent processes of the ecosphere and the linear, innovative, but ecologically disharmonious processes of the technosphere.' This mismatch is a part of the structural logic of capitalism so far as the environment is concerned. This is where the roots of the major ecological problems lie; these problems are inseparable from, indeed systemically determined by the conditions of existence of capitalism. That is why a general social definition of the environmental crisis, and therefore the delineation of the effective measures to avert it have to start from an understanding of the structural logic of the capitalist mode of production.

This is how Joel Kovel has put it:

> We should not, therefore, look for 'development,' nor 'corporations,' nor 'mistakes,' nor 'industrialisation,' nor 'technology,' nor 'greed,' nor 'consumerist lifestyles,' as being at the heart of the ecological crisis. Nor are population, patriarchy, or the basic philosophical attitudes of Western civilization central, either. All these things are implicated, but none of them occupies that place where the concrete determinants come together. We find, rather, when we explore that center, that it is occupied by the elusive entity known as *capital*, which to Marx was the 'all-dominating economic power of bourgeois society.' It is capital that conditions and drives separate determinations in an

ecologically destructive way, and so becomes the efficient cause of the crisis. Development, or industrialization, as such, is an empty construct. But development or industrialization under capitalist aegis, in which capitalist corporations, markets, lifestyles, even psychologies and character structure, all interact, is what destabilizes eco-system all over the planet.

VI

Capitalism is not some neutral process of technological progress for satisfaction of human needs. It is the production of goods and services for the profit of those who own the means by which they are produced. The realisation of profits for the few and the satisfaction of the needs of the majority rarely coincide. When they do, it is only indirectly, merely accidental, not structural, which, however, does not rule out the *manufacture* of satisfaction-seeking wants in a manner that creates new opportunities for profit-making. Whatever the pace at which capitalism spread or took over, it was relentlessly consistent in imposing its governing principle: the pursuit of profit through the market. The desire to maximise profits in the short run dominates all capitalist enterprise. It has to, and any capitalist who refuses to play the game according to this principle will be eliminated. The famous 'entrepreneur' of bourgeois economic science, all those corporate managers and the rest, are mere cogs in the wheel of the capitalist system. As Noam Chomsky once put it: 'The Chairman of the board will always tell you that he spends his every waking hour labouring so that people will get the best possible products at the cheapest possible price and work in the best possible conditions. But it is an institutional fact, independent of who the chairman of the board is, that he'd better be trying to maximize profit and market share, and if he doesn't do that, he's not going to be chairman of the board any more. If he were ever to succumb to the delusions that he expresses, he'd be out.' The competitive struggle between capitalists necessitates on pain of extinction the allocation of accumulated wealth to new, revolutionary technologies that serve to expand production so that profits continue to be made. It is thus that capitalists pursue their own interests, checked only by their mutual competition, and controlled in the short run by the impersonal forces of the market and in the long run, when the market fails – that is, the process of constantly expanding production and profit-making is interrupted – by devastating crises, compelling capitalist states to intervene to save capitalism from itself.

In their single-minded pursuit of profit, in which none can refuse to join on pain of elimination, capitalists are continuously driven to produce and sell and make more profit, to accumulate even more capital, and this becomes both their subjective goal and the motor force of the entire system. It is thus that in order to prosper, capitalist economies, as they have evolved in modern times, have to grow continuously, to grow for the sake of growth as it were, and accumulate. For capitalism, as Marx had pointed out: 'Accumulate, accumulate! That is Moses and the prophets!' It is this obsession with capital accumulation that distinguishes capitalism from the neutral, ahistorical technological progress or the simple system for satisfying human needs it is portrayed as in mainstream economic theory and by its ideologues and political representatives. And this obsession is a decisively causative factor in the current environmental crisis.

Driven by the structurally inherent need to accumulate, capitalism is a system that can never stand still. It is, as it were, trapped in an unending and uncontrollable cycle of expansion, experienced by every single manager of a capitalist enterprise as the imperative to 'Grow or Die' – in other words, keep up the rate of profit or be replaced by a more profitable competitor. If the investment frontier does not expand, and if profits do not increase and accumulation does not take place, the circulation of capital will be interrupted and a crisis will ensue. A 'stationary' capitalism is thus an impossibility. As Schumpeter expressed it, 'capitalism is a process, stationary capitalism would be a *contradictio in adjecto*'. Marx had pointed out (in *Communist Manifesto*) that 'constant revolutionising of production.... distinguishes the bourgeois epoch from earlier ones', that 'the bourgeoisie cannot exist without constantly revolutionising the instruments of production'. That is how capitalism is for ever changing and innovating, adopting new and discarding old methods of production and distribution, opening up new territories, subjecting to its purposes societies too weak to protect themselves – all the time looking for new sources or avenues of profit-making. Caught up in this process of restless innovation and expansion, the system rides roughshod over even its own beneficiaries if they get in its way or fall by the roadside. With profiteering and private accumulation as *the* thrust of the economic system, issues like ecological balance, sustainable growth or regional planning lose all significance. The economic interests are pursued with little thought and less concern for the effects on either society as a whole or the natural environment which the system draws on for the essentials of its own existence. One consequence is continuous degradation of environment, the environmental crisis of our times.

The issue here is important enough to be looked at more closely.

VII

Capitalism is an inherent threat to natural environment because of the primacy it gives to the profit motive. With its lack of concern for any priorities other than those of capital itself, capitalism perceives nature not as something to be also cherished and enjoyed but only as a mere resource or instrument, as something to be used, along with the human working class, as a means to the paramount ends of profit-making, and still more capital accumulation. A profit-oriented, market-governed economic development will always be anti-ecological. Even otherwise unlimited economic growth in a limited natural environment is a recipe for disaster. Interlocked within capitalism as a system, as Marx and Engels had pointed out, are the enormously powerful drives to both creation and destruction. The creative drive has found vivid expression in the extraordinary development of human and material productive forces, in what humankind has been able to get out of nature for its own uses. The destructive drive has now, among other things, come to bear most heavily on nature's capacity to respond to the demands placed on it. Capitalism with its fetishism of 'economic growth', its limitless greed and limitless consumption, its uncontrolled momentum and heedless rapacity, has brought humanity to a point where its powers of intervention in nature risk the destruction of the habitability of the globe.

It has been long recognised that capitalism as a system is loaded with major structural contradictions. A major contradiction was theorised by Marx, who recognised that in the endless search for profit, capitalists drive down the cost of labour, thus creating systematic poverty and unemployment in the midst of plenty, and setting recurrent economic crises into motion. Marx, even as he pointed out the degradation of 'conditions of production' this involved, also recognised and expressed concern over the damage capitalism inflicts on nature. Capitalist ravaging of humankind and nature has continued to be noted by sensitive economists and social analysts after him. Karl Polanyi, for example, in his *The Great Transformation*, specifically mentioned 'the devastation of the environment, deforestation, the pollution of rivers, the degradation of labour'. But the phenomena never came to be seriously theorised. Now the deepening ecological crisis has led scholars to posit this double ravaging as another major contradiction in the working of capitalism. James O'Connor has theorised it as capitalism's tendency to degrade the 'conditions of production' in its hunt for profit. These conditions, which include land (that is, non-human nature), labour power (the sustenance of which takes place through the bodies and communities of workers), and urban infrastructure, are treated like commodities although not produced as such, and in driving down their cost capitalism also degrades them.

It may be added that capitalism's tendency to plunder and vitiate the human, social and natural conditions of production by treating these conditions as commodities even though they are not produced as commodities, has now surfaced with ever more devastating effects as capitalism has gone on to 'globalise', that is, sought to 'restructure' itself in response to the current crisis of its accumulation process, and done so when this destructive tendency has now been freed up by the weakening or dismantling of 'Keynesian welfare-regulatory regimes' in the West, the collapse of 'actually existing socialism' in the East, and the failure of 'semi-autarkic models of nationalist socio-economic development and regulation' in the South – all of which have been displaced by neo-liberal 'free market' regimes, which place fewer social restraints on profit-driven production, trade, and finance. Global capitalism is attempting to rescue itself from its deepening crisis by cutting costs, by raising the rate of exploitation of labour, and by depleting and exhausting natural resources. Cost cutting has involved decreasing attention to working people's health and safety and increasing disregard of the global environment. Capitalism's intensified externalisation of social and environmental costs has meant not only rising misery and suffering of common people in all parts of the world, especially the South, but also led to increased pollution and global warming, further thinning of ozone layer, toxification of whole new regions, intensified withering away of rain forests and wild life and new threats of drought and disease. The ecological crisis is daily being aggravated as a result of the way capitalism has reorganised itself to get through its latest economic crisis.

It is necessary to emphasise that our assessment of capitalism and its consequences for the environment holds even if we assume that capitalists in their role as private citizens are highly moral individuals, who would never knowingly pollute the environment, employ harmful technologies or otherwise add to the burdens placed on the environment by a highly developed productive apparatus. At issue are not individuals, capitalists or any other, but the inescapable logic of capitalism with its inherent, profit-propelled compulsions to perpetual expansion and accumulation. It is not merely that capitalism is a system in which, in Rachel Carson's words, 'the right to make money, at whatever cost to others, is seldom challenged'. It is a necessary condition of capitalist survival that every human value be subordinated to this 'right', to the requirements of profit-maximisation, capital accumulation and 'growth' defined as the self-expansion of capital. There is an obvious contradiction between the short-term perspective of capital in its ceaseless quest for profit and the longer, wider view required to protect the environment. Even industries that have to look ahead must, sooner rather than later, satisfy the demands of investors, bond holders and banks for profit. The profit-seeking destruction of the planet's unrenewable resources is indeed one of the untranscendable limits of the capitalist system.

These limits, or structural logic of capitalism, is the reason why the much pleaded for 'environmental ethic' cannot take off in a capitalist society. It is not merely that capitalism perforce has an entirely contrary, appropriately its own, utilitarian ethic – 'possessive individualism', as Macpherson has called it. It is also that the most important assumption underlying it is substantially false, the assumption of capitalist as a free individual, free to chose and act, to opt for an 'environmental ethic'. This is not to be entirely dismissive about his freedom. Replacing the organic-static feudal society, capitalism came up as an atomistic but dynamic social formation; dynamic because of its atomism or individualism: old bonds dissolved, man was now free to pursue his self-interest in the marketplace, build a whole new world for himself. Though it involved the loss of the feudal era notion of social function, this individualism – celebrated in the utilitarian ethic and buttressed by the notion of God as 'G.T.' (the 'Great Taskmaster') who would now on help only those who help themselves – was a determining factor behind the extraordinary dynamism that characterised early capitalism, making it, then and later, a system more dynamic than all the earlier modes of production. Yet, for all his dynamism, capitalist has never been so free as bourgeois economic or social theory makes him out to be. Marx had early pointed out that he was yet subject to the 'blind forces' of the market. Or as Meszaros has recently put it, there is a price that, paradoxically must be paid for 'this incommensurable totalising dynamism of capitalism: 'the *loss of control* over the decision-making processes', which applies not only to the workers, in whose case the loss of control – whether in paid employment or out of it – is, rhetoric of 'free economic choice' notwithstanding, quite obvious, but even to the richest capitalists. They too must obey the objective imperatives of the system as a whole, or suffer the consequences and go out of business. Adam Smith himself had no illusions whatsoever in this regard when he chose to describe the real controlling power of the system as '*the invisible hand*'. The capitalist, thus, is simply not free to opt for an 'environmental ethic'. There can be no 'caring capitalists', capitalists in control of economic processes and free to take care of the environment.

To conclude, a system governed by the logic of profit maximisation and capital accumulation, capitalism is simply incapable of making its peace with the environment. Indeed, ecological vandalism is not an excess or excrescence of capitalism, index of a failure on its part. On the contrary, it is a token of success, the inevitable by-product of a system whose constitutive principle is the subordination of all human values to the drive for accumulation and requirements of profitability. Capitalism is by its very nature inimical to environment. This, it may be added, is the fundamental reason why a solution to the environmental crisis within capitalism is impossible, why environmental decline has not been stemmed so far. As experience has already shown, any expectation that capitalism can be made what is called 'friendly' to the environment, favourable to its sustainable use now and saving it for the future use of human species, is hopeless. International conferencing and treaty-making since the Earth Summit at Rio has made this clear again and again. Powerful capitalist interests have simply refused to countenance any such efforts. If, describing them as 'harmful' to its economy, the United States has led in opposing and rejecting even the modest demands of the global environmental movement, it has only confirmed its larger role as the leading defender of capitalism in the world.

(Incidentally, if capitalism, its production relations, have led to an increasingly destructive, including environment-destructive use of the forces of production, some of these forces, though necessarily socially embedded in capitalism, have acquired an autonomous, almost trans-historical, destructive character of their own, not only in the particular sense of arms manufacture, or *serving* the military-industrial complex, or in-built obsolescence, but in a far wider sense. These would include not only the malformed human beings of market societies but new productive techniques deformed by the fact that they are not necessary for economic growth or satisfaction of human needs but are exclusively a product of capitalists' interest in increased profit and market share. Thus deformed by capitalist production relations, quite often, 'environmental degradation is built into the technical design of (these) modern instruments of production', as Barry Commoner has pointed out – they are damaging not only to the present but the future as well. Environmental safety demands a change in the nature of such productive forces. This change however is not possible within capitalism or possible for capitalists to carry out. On the contrary, abolition of capitalism, of capitalist relations of production, is a necessary condition for their alteration or elimination. Their restructuring or elimination will in fact be among the major specific tasks of the succeeding socialist regime.)

VIII

The major responsibility for today's environmental crisis lies, as we have already noticed, with the advanced capitalist countries of the first world, with their economies geared to what in recent decades has come to be described as the 'American way of life' or 'throw-away lifestyle' – a lifestyle based, above all, on insatiable consumption. The essence of this lifestyle was well summed up by American retailing analyst Victor Labon when, shortly after World War II, he declared: 'Our enormously productive economy.... demands that we make consumption our way of life, that we convert the buying and use of goods into rituals, that we seek our spiritual satisfaction, or ego satisfaction, in consumption.... We need things consumed, burned up, worn out, replaced, and discarded at an ever increasing rate.' Four decades later, in 1993, underlining the damage this 'consumerism' does to the environment, the Worldwatch Institute, in its report on *State of the World,* said: 'The consumer life-style born in America and now emulated by a billion people worldwide causes the lion's share of ecological ills'.

Consumer culture or throw-away lifestyle of first world countries indeed imposes a heavy load on the global environment. Give or take a few per cents, the first world or the industrialised North, with 25 per cent of the world's population and owning 86 per cent of the world's industry, consumes 80 per cent of world energy. In comparison, the third world or the South, with 75 per cent of the world's population, owns only 14 per cent of world industry and consumes just 20 per cent of world energy. Globally, 20 per cent of the world's people in the rich countries account for 86 per cent of the total private consumption expenditures – the poorest 20 per cent located in the poor countries a miniscule 1.3 per cent. On a per capita basis, each resident of the advanced industrial countries consumes at least three times as much water, 10 times as much energy, 13 times as much iron and steel, 14 times as much paper, 18 times as much chemicals and 19 times as much aluminium as someone in a developing country like China or India. The first world consumes more packaging or toilet paper per capita than many poor countries can afford for school-books and newspapers. Consequently the industrial countries of the first world or the North account for nearly two-thirds of global emissions of carbon dioxide from the combustion of fossil fuels (carbon dioxide is the principal greenhouse gas). They account for three quarters of emissions of sulphur and nitrogen oxides that cause acid rain. Their factories generate most of the hazardous chemical wastes. Their air conditioners, aerosol sprays, and factories release almost 90 per cent of the chlorofluorocarbons that destroy the ozone layer. Their consumerist life style – the cars, disposable goods, packaging, high-fat diet, air-conditioning, etc. – depends on enormous and continuous inputs of the very commodities that are most damaging to the Earth to produce: energy, chemicals, metals, and paper. Overall, these countries are responsible for roughly 80 per cent of global pollution of all kinds.

The United States, with its 'conspicuous consumerism' and economy of automobiles, disposables, junk mail, space shuttles and high-tech weaponry, and unmatched generation of waste in all its forms, leads in this global pollution. As Alan Thein Durning, author of *How Much Is Enough?: The Consumer Society and the Future of the Earth,* has put it: 'Our cars, suburbs, shopping malls, throw-away products, meat and junk-food diet, add up to the most environmentally destructive way of life yet devised'. And this way of life is being 'sold' to people as never before. In 1992 alone U.S. business is known to have spent nearly 1 trillion dollars on marketing, that is, persuading and convincing people to consume more and more goods. This exceeded by almost 600 billion dollars the amount spent on education – public and private – at all levels. It is not surprising that more than 93 per cent of teenage girls questioned in a survey conducted in the late 1980s indicated that their favourite leisure activity was to go shopping!

In the 1950s William Vogt had charged that the United States, with one-sixteenth of the world's population, was utilising one-third of the globe's resources. Later, towards the end of 1980s, the environmentalist NGO *Zero Population Growth* estimated that each American consumed thirty times as much resources as an Indian. More recently, the United States, with around 5 per cent of the world's population, has been estimated to consume 20 per cent (or some such disproportionate share) of the world's non-renewal natural resources. The U.S. gobbles up a quarter of the world's energy supplies, about as much energy as used by the entire third world. Martin Khor Kok Peng of the Third World Network has pointed out: 'New Yorkers use more energy commuting in a week than the energy used by all Africans for all uses in a year'. According to recent calculations by John Young of the World Watch Institute, the average American accounts for the use of some 540 tons of construction materials, 18 tons of paper, 23 tons of wood, 16 tons of metals, and 32 tons of organic chemicals in the course of a lifetime, and he points out that this is unsustainable, not so much because we are likely to run out of the needed raw materials, but because the processes used to produce them court human and ecological catastrophe. America discharges ten times more carbon dioxide per capita than, for example, China. It is today by far the largest producer of greenhouse gases, accounting for 25 per cent of the world total, and, therefore, most responsible for the threat now posed by global warming. United States is indeed the world's most voracious resource consumer, even as the first world as a whole wallows in its mindless consumerism and thus pollutes and ravages the global environment.

It has been rightly suggested that the starting point of ecological rectification, the much argued-for sustainable development, should be the capitalist countries of the first world which, through their present high levels of consumption and polluting technologies damage not only their own environment but that of the rest of the world as well. Furthermore, it is well-established that it is the working classes, oppressed minorities, women, and the rural and urban poor worldwide who suffer most from both economic and ecological exploitation. The burden of ecological destruction indeed falls most disproportionately on the poor, which again suggests that the idea of sustainable development has a meaning only if it starts with the affluence and the unsustainability of the rich in the advanced capitalist countries. But it is typical of capitalism that, compelled to face the worsening environmental situation, it sees this less as a problem to be overcome than one to be managed in accordance with the logic of the free market which, in effect, means passing the costs of environmental crisis on to the more vulnerable sections within the advanced affluent societies and even more to the poor people of the third world. It is a fact that in all class-divided societies, governments constantly make decisions – in regard to health, education, working conditions, housing, and social services in general – that are based on difference in valuation among classes, though they rarely care to admit it or defend their policies in this way. Indeed such differences in valuation, as anyone with the slightest knowledge of history and economics would know, are at the very core of capitalist economy and the state, within countries and on a global scale. Capitalism's policies on environment are no exception. It is not surprising therefore to find heavily polluting operations at home located in poor neighbourhoods, where live the counterparts of the world poor within the rich countries. This is in fact a common practice, and the United States is again an exemplar. In 1983 a study by the U.S. General Accounting Office determined that three out of the four off-site commercial hazardous landfills in the southern states were located in primarily black communities even though blacks represented only 20 per cent of the population in the region. Other studies have confirmed that most hazardous waste dumps in the U.S. are located near poor African-American and Latino communities. The disproportionate presence of pollution and toxic sites in communities of colour all across the country is now well recognised as 'environmental racism' which has only added to the ghetto misery of the poor in the United States.

On a global scale, again, the votaries of sustainable development should be addressing themselves to the production and consumption pattern in the advanced capitalist countries which is leading to destruction of natural resources in the world. Instead of blaming the third world for depleting common resources, they need to pay heed to what Fidel Castro said at the Rio summit:

> A consistent interpretation of sustainable development should begin with the recognition that underdevelopment is the result of plundering of the third world, which has been prolonged in our time by an international economic order that uses the mechanism of debt, unfair division of the world's labour, trade protectionism and control over the flow of finances to heighten the exploitation of the underdeveloped nations, and as a consequence, the ensuing ecological degradation.

In other words, it is first and foremost the first world which needs to subject its own industrial structure and technology to the conditions of survival of humanity. But what we are witnessing is really a globalisation of policies and practices already evident in the U.S. and which have recently been unearthed in locations throughout the advanced capitalist world. That is, the third world, which has long helped maintain consumption levels in the first world, whose underconsumption is already a structural counterpart of the overconsumption in the first world – the latter indeed owes 'unlimited ecological debt' to the third world for maintaining its affluence – is now being cast in the role of the main victim of the ecological ravages of global capitalism and used as the site for polluting industries and a dumping ground for the dangerous toxic wastes in the first world. A Nimbi – Not-in-My-Backyard – syndrome is at work which has meant ecologically unsustainable development projects, including hazardous industries, shifting out of the advanced capitalist North to the underdeveloped South. For the rest, population growth in the South has become the target of the debate on sustainable development with the obvious interest of obscuring or watering down North's own responsibility for the destruction of global environment.

IX

One of Marx's most enduring insights about capitalism is his observation about its structurally-compelled thrust to expand abroad, a thrust which has no regard for national boundaries. This has been well expressed in capitalism's long-standing, peaceful or violent, pursuit of cheap raw materials, cheap labour, low taxes, and captive markets all over the world, an accumulation of capital on a world scale, accompanied by a wave of plunder and pillage unparalleled in history, producing the 'wealth' of the over-developed consumer societies of the west insofar as it is not a mirage for the bulk of their population; its victims being not only the peoples of the third world, but men and women of the future as well. For imperialist expansion and exploitation, whatever its different forms, has always carried with it direct or indirect threat to the environment, hitherto hidden dangers to life and health everywhere, most of all in the third world.

The direct threat has been most manifest in the wars waged by capitalist-imperialist powers. It comes through most vividly in the U.S. war against Vietnam, which was a war against the environment as well as against people with chemical and biological weapons symbolised by, but not limited to, the use of Agent Orange. Vietnam's experience, with its linkages of imperialism, ecological destruction and modern warfare shows that imperialism not only despoils the environment in its pursuit of profits in the third world, but also that modern imperialist warfare, based as it so often is on indiscriminate aerial bombing, is a major source of environmental destruction. The war on the Sandinista government in Nicaragua and wars on Iraq and Afghanistan are other recent examples that immediately come to mind. Apart from the oil spill in the first Gulf war, the depleted uranium weapons used by the U.S. and Britain are known to have left 40 tons of radioactive debris in the desert, having the potential of causing hundreds of thousands of deaths in future. The notable point about this direct threat is its imposition of environmental costs primarily on countries of the third world. This is equally true of the indirect threat carried by imperialist expansion. The indirect environmental damage is part of the history of colonialism as the transformation of the colonies to serve the interest of colonial powers. For example, there was the transformation of agriculture from its natural complexity (and diversity of crops) to the simplicity of commodified agriculture. The pressure of producing for the world market rendered many third world agricultures vulnerable not only to the fluctuations of the global economy, but to environmentally destructive farming techniques as well. European colonialism of the Malay World saw the region becoming the foremost producer of tin, rubber and timber for the world market – something achieved through large scale deforestation and excavation of the earth. The clearing of the forest lands for export crops dates to the Spanish conquest in Latin America, rightly labelled by Faber as 'ecological imperialism'.

Neo-colonialism of recent times has continued this degradation and ravaging of the environment in the third world. A good example is the ravaging of forests by some of the world's largest corporations which has been documented by Joshua Karliner in his *The Corporate Planet: Ecology and Politics in the Age of Globalisation*. The US-based transnationals are of course at the forefront of this ravaging, but they are hardly alone. Japan's Mitsubishi Corporation, the world's largest corporation (with revenues exceeding $173 billion), has been called 'the worst destroyer of rainforests in the world' by the Rainforest Action Network (RAN). According to Karliner, the company harvests rainforest logs in Malaysia, markets plywood from Indonesia, participates in the joint venture Eidai do Brasil, 'one of the largest milling operations in the Brazilian Amazon', chops down tropical forests throughout the Bolivian Amazon, 'including endangered mahogany', and otherwise overwhelms the Chilean forests 'traditionally occupied by indigenous Mapuche communities' by converting sylvan paradise 'into ecologically destructive monocrop eucalyptus plantations'. Meanwhile, in North America, Mitsubishi stands as 'one of the largest wood exporters from the Pacific Northwest', and in Alberta, Canada, 'is the majority owner of the largest chlorine bleach pulp and paper mill in the world'. Additionally, Mitsubishi and the US-based transnational Weyerhaeuser have taken up the mass export of logs from Siberia, where clear-cuts of forest habitat now threaten extinction for the Siberian tiger.

The colonial and neo-colonial ravaging of third world environment is now generally acknowledged. But as capitalism, governed as always by its logic of capital accumulation, pursues its goals in the age of globalisation, a notable new development has taken place. To its worldwide scramble for resources and markets and outlets for profitable investment, which has already taken the form of technological anomalies, unregulated chemical hazards and environmental degradation, sporadic war and chronic hunger in the third world, global capitalism has recently added a specific new objective: a search for the most regulation-free sites for environmental destruction, whether in the form of deforestation, pesticide poisoning, dangerous industrial processes, or toxic waste dumps. The result is an arrangement in which the most severe scourges of the system – in the environmental as in other matters – often emerge at great distances from the metropolis, in the third as also the former second world.

An 'environmental colonialism' has emerged, not only as capitalism's answer to the environmental crisis, but to ensure conditions conducive to continued world accumulation of capital, which is finding its victims once again in the third world in view of its lack of economic independence and vulnerability to the pressure of global capitalism. While the affluent countries of the first world, most responsible for the global environmental crisis, have refused to accept any major sacrifice on their part, issues are so posed as to demand that in the interests of saving the environment, the poor third world countries – where some two-thirds (or more) of the world's population lives in sub-human conditions – forsake most, if not all their aspirations to economic development. South has been asked to slow down its development in the name of 'global interdependence'. Even the survival needs of its poor are questioned. The destruction of rain forests in Brazil is condemned and the people are asked to keep off the forests to save them, ignoring the fact that the people in Brazil also must eat and they need not only forest produce but also new farmland. It is a specificity of the environmental debate today that the poor, marginalised people in the third world are in conflict with forces that seek to deny their aspirations to a better life, even deprive them of their livelihood.

As in most matters elsewhere, bourgeois hypocrisy abounds in the field of environment too. In international conferences, developed capitalist nations like the U.S. take third world countries to task for not doing enough to save the environment and at the same time multinationals of these nations routinely dump toxic wastes and shift their polluting industries to poor African, Latin American or Asian countries. The issue of third world deforestation is globalised while the far more important issue of the energy-intensive lifestyle in the first world is marginalised. The discussion over the 'greenhouse effect' evades the crucial problem of controlling the burning of heavy amounts of fossil fuel in the rich capitalist countries while world attention is focussed on the less important contribution of local tropical deforestation including by the poor in search of their livelihood. The solution of global warming is identified as a halt in Amazonian deforestation while even a conservative estimate projects a doubling of carbon dioxide concentration in the atmosphere in about 50 years, mainly from the industrially advanced capitalist countries.

The third world countries, as in the past, remain necessary

to global capitalism's capital accumulation process, but this time they are also needed for setting up polluting industries, exporting drugs and pesticides not considered safe for use at home, and as dumping grounds for nuclear and other dangerous wastes – 'garbage imperialism' it has been called. Beginning with Africa as the first victim of toxic waste export schemes, the third world has been the worst victim of such dumping. The developed countries ship an estimated 20 million tons of waste to the third world each year. There can be few more blatant examples of the continuing dominance of imperialism over third world affairs. (As detailed by a Greenpeace report entitled 'Russia: The Making of a Waste Colony', Russia too has been, rather tragically, a large dumping ground for hazardous and toxic wastes in recent years. In the words of a Greenpeace spokesman, 'Western Europe is practising a kind of environmental colonialism in Russia'. Which, incidentally, is as good an indication as any of the place of post-Soviet Russia in the world of global capitalism).

The ideology and value system of this new phase of capital accumulation found a rare and remarkably honest expression in an internal memorandum within the World Bank, submitted by its then chief economist Lawrence Summers towards the end of 1991 – leaked and published soon after in *The Economist* under the significant title 'Let Them Eat Pollution'. In the *Economist's* view Summers' language may be objectionable but 'his economics was hard to answer'. Holding that 'underdeveloped countries are vastly underpolluted', that there is need for 'intelligent discrimination' concerning environmental standards to be applied in different parts of the world, that 'the economic logic behind dumping a load of toxic waste in the lowest-wage country is impeccable', Summers argued in favour of 'encouraging *more* migration of the dirty industries to the LDCs (less developed countries)' because they could absorb more pollution. Life expectancies already short and wages low, people here had so much less to lose from dying young. Few doubt that the central argument of Summers' memo was a serious one and still holds, and few among the orthodox economists would disagree with its views on the environment, reflecting as they do the logic of capital accumulation in our times. Even otherwise bourgeois economists think exactly like this when they value a human life as the present value of the future wage stream, and do the appropriate cost-benefit calculations on that basis. Summers indeed concluded that social and humanitarian arguments against such migration of polluting industries and trade in toxic wastes can be disregarded since they are the same arguments that are used against all proposals for capitalist development.

Though admittedly 'heartless' in tone, Summers' memo only spelled out what is implied in the environmental politics of the rich capitalist countries. And what is implied is frightening in its total, utterly cynical, disregard for human values. It is not only that worldwide costs of production would fall if polluting industries were shifted from the centre to the periphery of the world capitalist system and therefore such shifting is justified, but also that the lives of individuals in the 'low wage', 'vastly underpolluted' third world are worthless, hundreds of times less than that of individuals in advanced capitalist countries where wages are often hundred times higher, and that a clean environment is a luxury good to be possessed only by rich countries with high life expectancies where higher aesthetic and health standards apply.

The most shocking part of the Summers' memo was not only the openly exploitative attitude that it demonstrates towards the world's poor, but also the utter contempt it displays both for them and the world environment. But this policy perspective is no intellectual aberration. It reflects the fact that while the first world still needs the third world, it has reached a new understanding (that rests on a new technology) in which such people are no longer valued as labour power to be exploited. They are nothing but an impediment and a potential danger – not a relatively surplus population, but an absolutely surplus population which is best got rid off. This understanding itself is part of a larger ideological orientation, wherein the first world claims the 'right to interfere' in the third world in defence of its interests. That is how we have a professor of Community Medicine at the Leeds University, Maurice King, advocating –

as a solution to the 'population problem' – a drastic curtailing of the rehydration therapy and immunisation programmes in the third world which save millions of infants from early death – aptly described by Halfdan Mahler (former DG, WHO) as mass euthanasia of children in the poor countries of the South to maintain a sustainable eco-system; or the World Health Forum initiating a Round Table around an article by one Jean Martin advocating a shift from Hippocratic medical ethics to a Machiavellian one. Neither the welfare nor the lives of the majority of the population of the globe, nor the ecological fate of the earth – not even the fate of individual capitalists themselves – can be allowed to stand in the way of making profits and keep the process of capital accumulation going. Nothing is more characteristic of bourgeois ideology today, or of bourgeois economics, or for that matter the logic of capital accumulation itself. Needless to add, it is all very much in the classic pattern of imperialism.

This, however, does not obviate the need for the third world to address its environmental crisis through means that do not reinforce the imperialist hegemony. It has even been suggested, and quite rightly, that the third world could take advantage of its backwardness and underdevelopment, its 'late-arrival' on the scene so to speak, to avoid repeating many of the pitfalls and disasters of capitalist-led economic development in the west. It could not only take advantage of the advanced scientific knowledge currently available and adopt the best of scientifically rational and environmentally benign technologies, but also use and develop the traditional, environment-friendly technologies in an economically, socially and environmentally rational planned economy based on considerations other than profit. That is, opt for a sustainable development which also caters to the needs of the vast majority. This option, however, seems lost, at least for the time being. Post-decolonisation, the third world countries have evolved their own more or less developed class-exploitative systems or country-specific peripheral capitalisms. As 'developing' countries – developing along which path? – they have ended up taking, in Mao's words, 'the capitalist road', which is also the road to environmental degradation. Post-Soviet collapse and facing the offensive of recharged global capitalism, they have turned over their economies still more to capitalists, corporations and the free markets so that what gets developed is simply what is profitable, with no concern for the well-being of the people at large or the environment. As 'the lucky beneficiaries of West's transfer of technology', they are home to west's 'smoke-stack industries' moving abroad to escape 'green harassment' as it is called, which has only added to their environmental problems. As the globalised elites wallow in throw-away consumerism, 'the American way of life', its junk food and junk culture including anti-state hysteria and glorification of individualism, the common people bear the cost of it all in the form of polluted environment. The governments do concede gravity of the situation from time to time, but insist that pollution is a global problem, that the main responsibility for cleaning it up should fall on the developed countries, that if the developed countries wanted the developing countries to adopt clean technologies, they should provide financial assistance for technology transfer – which is a reasonable and justifiable position to take. They also charge the foreign-funded NGOs with burdening them with 'environmentalism' in the interests of developed countries, and the charge is not without merit. But most often these are excuses to carry on just as they are. There is a great deal of ad hoc governmental noise and discursive activity over environment, producing small improvements, but there is little recognition that a capitalist or market organisation of the economy is simply incompatible with environmental safety or sustainable development. In short, nature of the economy and the balance of class forces in the third world make impossible any kind of effective response to its environmental problems. Rooted in class exploitation, poverty and the unequal control of resources and political power, the environmental crisis only continues to deepen in the third world. Its ruling classes or elites, responsible for degrading the environment of their countries on their own are also willing or unwilling collaborators as global capitalism now despoils and ravages the third world environment.

As stated above, all this is in the classic pattern of

imperialism. But its ecological dimension, the magnitude of the environmental threat involved has given a new twist to the situation which, though implicit in our argument, needs to be specifically noted. In earlier times, the ravages of imperialism had no directly adverse effect on the metropolitan population, unless of course the direct victims actually rose in revolt, provoking costly intervention. What is new and needs to be explicitly stated is that with the environmental crisis nature has even less regard for national borders than does capitalism. Toxic wastes, petroleum pollution, and deforestation – not to mention processes more confined to advanced capitalist countries, such as the use of CFCs – have a global impact. The advanced affluent countries themselves can no longer escape the directly adverse consequences of their ravages abroad. The achievements of capitalism in one portion of the world and the devastation it has wrought elsewhere, have come to be linked through destruction of the environment, thereby threatening the very survival of humankind on this earth. This is both a feature of capitalism today and an argument for its replacement by socialism.

X

It is necessary to understand capitalism, specifically the dynamics of capital accumulation, in order to understand why environmental degradation happens and will continue to happen in the capitalist world. Failure to see this structural dimension of the problem, the integral relation between ecological crisis and capitalism is indeed the major weakness of the contemporary movement in defence of ecology and environment. There is wide consciousness about the environmental degradation around us, of the disastrous consequences if it continues. But there is very little understanding that this is the natural, a necessary, result of capitalism. Even those who do not view the implementation of specific environment-protection measures as the be-all and end-all of their activity, refer rather vaguely to some 'unsustainable pattern of development', and soon end up locating the cause of the environmental crisis in the near-natural process of 'industrialisation'. Their basic hypothesis is: the industrial societies of this earth are producing ecological problems and contradictions which must in the foreseeable future lead to their collapse. There is no effort to define the historical specificity of the 'industrialisation' of our times. That is also how the argument that what is needed is 'controlled growth' is completely beside the point. For the issue is not *whether* or *not* we produce under *some* control, but under what *kind* of control. Our present state of affairs, it needs to be recognised, has been produced under the 'iron-fisted control' that the logic of capital accumulation exercises over the economy. 'The costs of cleaning up our environment must be met in the end by the community' is another platitudinous response, which in its evasion of the real issue not only provides an alibi to the established socio-economic system for its degradation of environment but also wants the people to pay – through cuts in their standard of living, etc. – to keep this system going by meeting the costs of 'environmental rehabilitation' as it is called. Characteristic of our times is post-modernism's contribution to contemporary green theory which refuses to see that the cause of ecological degradation lies not in modernity or science, as it contends, but in the capitalist mode of production.

The more radical minority trends within the movement (like deep ecology, social ecology, bio-regionalism, eco-feminism, etc.), have offered some fundamental critiques of the prevailing order of things in the world. But this has not led them or persuaded the mainstream environmentalism to look deeper and historically and see the *capitalist* roots of the ongoing ecological crisis. They do see the excesses of 'possessive individualism' in the reckless profligacy of western consumerism, its luxury-related use of natural resources, but fail to relate it with capitalism. Ecological rationality is advocated but it is not realised that it is simply incompatible with capitalism's inner dynamics, the essential drive of 'industrialisation' that is capitalism, with its commitment to unlimited growth, the market as the sole criterion for orienting development, the enterprise as the sole subject of decision-making, and profit as the sole motive behind, and yardstick for measuring, results. In an ultimate sense, demands for large-scale ecological rationality are radical, their satisfaction requires fundamental structural change in society. This is not recognised by the environmental movement in its totality, with the result that there is no real connection between the environmental 'consciousness' and a political understanding of what really needs to be done or, more accurately, while the spread of environmental consciousness is there, the inadequacy or lack of depth of this consciousness is reflected in the inadequacy and lack of effectiveness of the environmental movement as a whole.

To put the argument more sharply, beyond its failure to recognise that it is not possible to deal with the problem of ecological degradation without a long-term analysis and evaluation of social production as a whole, that this degradation is not a problem of 'industry', 'technology' or 'modernisation' per se, independent of the historically specific social relations of production and exchange in our times, nor a problem of ideology to be solved by greater ecological awareness or changes in individual lifestyle, the major weakness of mainstream environmentalism lies in its failure to understand the *politics* of ecological concerns: that ecological degradation is a political problem in the sense that it is produced or determined by the differential control of resources and political power in society, a problem of undemocratic control over resources and decision-making processes among classes and nations and, therefore, incapable of resolution without altering this situation, without the power to establish democratic control over the production process, to plan research, investment and consumption in an eco-friendly manner – in short, power totally different from that which obtains under capitalism. To be really effective, the struggle for ecology and environment has to be conducted in this perspective, as part of the larger struggle for a social order radically different in its economic and political power structures from capitalism, so as to be not only democratic and humane but also ecologically rational, in other words, socialist in its principles.

Evidence, if needed, for the centrality of the question of

power and of structural change to ecological concerns, has recently come from a least expected but impeccably mainstream source, the prestigious Business Council for Sustainable Development whose members include a representative sample of the top officers of the world's biggest multinational corporations: Chevron Oil, Mitsubishi, Ciba-Geigy, Dow Chemical, and DuPont, to name a few. In a statement which would have been surprising a few years ago but can no longer be viewed as exceptional, the Council says: 'We cannot continue in our present methods of using energy, managing forests, farming, protecting plant and animal species, managing urban growth, and producing industrial goods. We certainly cannot continue to reproduce our own species at the present rate.'

What is significant is not only that such a sweeping assessment should have come from the controlling stratum of society which is responsible for the practices said to be driving us towards disaster, but that this assessment should be accompanied by a frank admission that those who are responsible and have the power to make changes are the very ones who have the least reason to want to do so. 'The painful truth', according to the Council, 'is that the present is a relatively comfortable place for those who have reached positions of mainstream political or business leadership. That is the crux of the problem of sustainable development, and perhaps the main reason why there has been great acceptance of it in principle, but less concrete action to put it into practice; many of those with the power to effect the necessary changes have the least motivation to alter the status quo that gave them that power'. This is honest enough but put rather simplistically. For what is at issue is not the personal inclinations of those in power but the nature of the power structure that put them there, a power structure which is based at every level, directly or indirectly, on making profits – not in some visionary future, but here and now, today and tomorrow. Those who refuse to play the game are soon eliminated or marginalised. In other words, they can hold on to their power only if they do not try to use it for purposes incompatible with the historically determined nature of the power structure itself, with the class interests of those dominant in a capitalist society. The conclusion is inescapable: the kind of power structure that prevails in most of the world today is incapable of meeting the most basic survival needs of the species. It needs to be changed, within countries and on a global scale, if there is to be any realistic hope for averting the looming eco-catastrophe and ensuring the long-term continuation of human civilisation on this earth.

It is this understanding of the politics of ecology that the environmentalist movement as a whole needs to acquire and act upon, linking its immediate struggles with the larger purpose of a necessary structural change in society, if it is to achieve success in its ultimate aim of saving the environment.

It is this understanding, rather this understanding of politics, which has been missing in the contemporary Green movement and its reform-oriented Green parties in the west. Hence their lack of achievement and growing marginalisation in recent years. Coming up with much fanfare and hope, these parties are ending up as so many appendages to an effete social democracy. Istvan Meszaros has observed:

> They appealed to individuals concerned about the ongoing environmental destruction, leaving undefined the underlying socioeconomic causes, as well as their class connotations. This they did precisely in order to broaden their own electoral appeal, in the hope of successfully intervening in the reform process for the purpose of reversing the identified dangerous trends. The fact that within a relatively short space of time all such parties became marginalised, despite their spectacular initial successes almost everywhere, underlines that the causes manifesting in environmental destruction are much more deep-seated than it was assumed by the leaders of these programmatically non-class oriented reform movements, including the people who imagined that they could institute a viable alternative to the socialist project by inviting its adherents to move 'From Red to Green'.
>
> No matter how important – indeed literally vital – as a 'single issue' around which varieties of the Green movement tried to articulate their reform programmes, so as to make an inroad into the power structure and decision making processes of the established order, the incontestable imperative of environmental protection turned out to be quite intractable on account of the corresponding necessary restraints which its implementation

would have to mean to the prevailing production processes. The capital system proved to be unreformable even under its most obviously destructive aspect.

Today the difficulty is not only that the dangers inseparable from the ongoing development are much greater than ever before, inasmuch as the global capital system had reached its contradictory zenith of maturation and saturation. The dangers now extend over the whole planet, and consequently the urgency of doing something about them before it is too late happens to be particularly acute. To aggravate the situation, everything is further complicated by the fact that it is not feasible to find partial solutions to the problems that must be faced. Thus no 'single issue' can be realistically considered a 'single issue'. If nothing else, this circumstance has been forcefully highlighted by the disconcerting marginalisation of the Green movement on the success of which so much hope has been placed in recent times, even among former socialists.

XI

The above argument does not mean that no ecologically beneficial changes can be made without changing the nature of the power structure or structural change in society. On the contrary, we must recognise the important contribution of the environmentalist movement, of ecologists, scientists and activist groups in securing such changes within the existing system. A great deal of useful work has been done and there can be nothing but admiration for some of the struggles waged. There is much untapped potential here and socialists need to participate in, support and encourage ongoing ecological movements and struggles. Fortunately for the world, capitalism has never been allowed to develop for long entirely in accordance with its own logic, the logic of the market. Popular opposition and working class struggles have often forced the system to moderate its worst tendencies, and the ensuing reforms, to some extent at least, have resulted in lasting beneficial constraints on the market. The same is true of the opposition and struggles in defence of the environment. There is no doubt that the efforts to check the excesses of capitalism, by its victims, by farsighted leaders of the capitalist state, by voluntary organisations and others have served to limit the more destructive depredations of uncontrolled capital. Without this, possibly, capitalism by now would have destroyed both its environment and itself.

The environmentalist movement, thus, has its achievements. But even on a generous interpretation these have been few and rather modest. It has certainly made for a remarkable spread of environmental consciousness. But high visibility at seminars and conferences, national and international, notwithstanding, the objective gains have been absolutely inadequate in terms of the needs of the situation. Far from securing any fundamental change, these can at best be said to have slowed down the rush to disaster, revealing once again the inherent limitations of all reformism within capitalism. This is not to deny that reformist measures are valuable, even necessary, insofar as they improve our survivability and teach us how to proceed. But they become a hindrance if we are misled into thinking that reform is sufficient in itself. There is everything to be said in defence of a struggle for reforms – it is indeed here that all struggle against capitalism begins – but it must not be viewed as an end in itself; to be ultimately effective the struggle must be conducted in a perspective of radical systemic change. Capitalism must go if environment has to be really saved and we are to survive as a civilisation, indeed as a species. All reforms and partial measures need to be taken in the spirit of bringing about capitalism's downfall.

This is precisely what has been by and large missing in the environmentalist movement as a whole. The social and political thinking of mainstream ecologists has been marred by a very limited vision of things, at times even plain naiveté. As activists, when they are not just NGO careerists, most of them rotate in a world of their own creation, innocent of questions of both economics and power. Cocooned in their 'environmentalism', the concept of 'capitalism' is unknown to them. They have no idea at all that if discussion of capitalism is ruled out, nothing very significant can be said about alleviating environmental degradation, let alone reversing the trend. They see this degradation as the product of 'errors' of policies which could be corrected, or 'mistaken values' which need to be changed. Many have been busy calling for a moral revolution that would incorporate ecological values into our culture and most of them have a missionary style, seeking converts to the cause, calling for an ethic of renunciation and self-limitation. Their calls and the style often smack of a preacher's sermon in which, as Hans Magnus Enzensberger once pointed out, 'the horror of the predicted catastrophe contrasts sharply with the mildness of the admonition with which we are allowed to escape'. We have only to look at the World Watch reports which generally limit recommendations to preaching good behaviour. There is much rhetoric and appeals to the rationality of their readers or listeners, whoever they may be – if only they would grasp what is at stake – but little realisation that it is not men or their lust for power, the leaders or even capitalists, but system and its logic that is the cause of the problem. The people are asked to consume less which ignores the culture of poverty, fear and scarcity within which most of the world's people live, and the culture of consumerism within which the people of capitalist societies are trapped. Both cultures make it functionally impossible to take a genuinely ecological attitude; and they are both deeply structured by the capitalist system. Reasonableness and compassion of capitalists is appealed to, which confuses the traits of individuals with those of the system they serve. A corporate leader who sees the ecological light will not change the system. He will simply stop being a corporate leader, to be replaced by someone who sees things as capitalism does. The individual is persistently asked to adopt new values and the people of the 'rich' lands to give up cars and otherwise lower their standard of living. It is surely necessary for individuals to struggle to so organise their lives that they live more simply and ecologically. But it is also a fact that this kind of personal conversion is not a simple matter of free choice. People, for example, even if they so wished, cannot give up wanting cars unless we have at least an adequate public transport system in place, to say nothing of having a community that allows us to live – in the full sense of this term – without one. Personal and structural changes are mutually reinforcing; neither can succeed without the other. And it is the need for structural change that is most continuously evaded. Proposals like a brake on population increase, de-development of the economy, draconian rationing, change in lifestyle and so on – these are all offered in a spirit of enlightened moral commonsense and to be carried out in a peaceful liberal manner, harming no interests or privileges, and demanding no changes in the social and political system. Indeed the unwillingness to consider any radical interference with the political system is a characteristic of mainstream environmentalism. Occasional talk of empowering the people notwithstanding, this system is taken as a constant factor. The result is a complete depoliticisation of the ecological question. Its social components and political dimensions never come to be considered seriously. The ecological protest almost always ends up with appeals for state intervention. The state indeed intervenes well-knowing how to protect the ruling class interests - it is always bountiful with promises of 'improvement in the quality of life', without of course indicating whose life is going to be made more beautiful, in what way and at whose expense. The ecological movement has at times indeed served to spruce up the environment, deodorise its stench, to make it pleasanter, less ugly, healthier and hence more tolerable for the privileged at the expense of the common people, their jobs and livelihood. Just as, at other times, in another form of cooptation, environmentalism gets reduced to 'fire-fighting', to a practice of rather modest crisis-management within capitalism, almost invariably with the help of the capitalist state. Only, in its failure to get at the core of the problem, this only reinforces that core and ultimately worsens the problem.

The activity of environmentalist groups is usually aimed at resolving a particular problem or crystallises around specific interests. It is successful in checking the construction of an oil refinery, a new nuclear plant or a dam here or reduction in the output of chlorofluorocarbons there, or getting anti-pollution norms set for cars elsewhere. But the construction takes place when the opposition slacks or shifts where resistance is weak; there is no cancellation of project or reduction in energy consumption or change in the energy or water management policies. This parallels the overall nature and outcome of state intervention which, without seriously impeding the workings of the market, secures the needed improvement in some intensively targeted spheres while deterioration continues unchecked elsewhere. (A good example is governmental policies in many developed and developing capitalist countries in recent decades, with their focus on controlling vehicular air pollution in selected urban centres while ecological degradation in general, including air pollution elsewhere or otherwise, continues.)

Typical of mainstream environmentalism are appeals to technocratic rationality, accompanied by proposals of 'putting scientists and experts at the top', and hopes for 'an environmental revolution' on the lines of the agricultural and industrial revolutions, which too will be driven by new technologies. This ignores the fact that the real issues in the environmental crisis are not scientific or technological but economic and political, which 'scientists and experts' – even as they have done so much to alert us to the dangers facing humanity, and the planet as we know it –are generally ill-equipped to understand and deal with. Today more and more scientists are indeed calling for government and multi-national intervention against the rapacity and destructiveness of the global market economy, through binding treaties to save the ozone layer, control global warming, check over-fishing, etc. In effect, this amounts to calling for a planned, rational use of global natural resources, that is, going beyond capitalism. But few scientists address the economy or capitalism's profit system directly. There are odd exceptions like the scientist-ecologist Barry Commoner, who has argued that any 'significant environmental improvement depends on social rather than private governance', that decisions which affect the entire society cannot be left to the whims of private owners of corporations, that society itself should have some democratic control over the economy. But most scientists and experts end up calling only for careful management, which leaves the social bases of environmental crisis, lying in capitalism, unquestioned and unaddressed. It may be added that managerial or technocratic rationality invariably has anti-democratic implications: environment rules and measures coming to be imposed on a population from the top. 'Ecology does not necessarily imply the rejection of authoritarian, techno-fascist solutions', as Andre Gorz has warned.

Along with stop-gap, possibly viable measures – like construction of the means of mass transport, erection of plants for the filtration and desalination of sea-water, use of new sources of energy, synthetic production of raw materials, more intensive agricultural techniques, etc. (which of course will create their own problems) – there is the largely theoretical advocacy of such radical changes as phasing out of fossil-burning energy industries, minimisation if not elimination of dependence on the automobile, replacement of a transportation system based on the internal combustion engine (which will necessitate a comprehensive relocation of producing and consuming centres), banning or drastic reduction of polluting technologies, etc. These are certainly among the 'necessary changes'. But what such advocacy misses is that such radical changes or reforms have obvious anti-capitalist implications, that they seek to impose an utterly new condition of caution and constraint on a system whose entire historical thrust has been in just the opposite direction, that a capitalism which could accommodate all this would not be capitalism at all. Essentially concerned with making and accumulating profits, capitalism cannot simply undergo a conversion and turn into a system concerned with saving the environment.

Sometimes an alternative is sought in decentralised, environmentally sound economy – one of small units, renewable energy sources, and non-polluting technologies, making for a community capable of building a clean environment and keeping it clean – a proposal deserving of serious and sympathetic consideration. It is true that the degradation of local ecological systems often do have local solutions in terms of prevention and a certain degree of de-linking. But most ecological problems as well as the economic problems which are both cause and effect of the ecological problems cannot be adequately addressed at the local level; the local responses need to be situated in regional, national, even international contexts. Popular movements confined to the community, municipality, or village cannot by themselves deal effectively with most of both the economic and ecological aspects of the general destructiveness of global capitalism, not to speak of the destructive dialectic between economic and ecological crises. Such movements or struggles have remained mostly 'populist' and 'localist' and thus incapable of countering capitalism's increasingly broad and deep, and destructive, exploitation of natural and social wealth. In the long run an isolated community effort within predominant capitalism is a utopian exercise, doomed to be a failure. For it to embrace the entire society requires a public authority strong enough to break up and overcome the capitalist concentrations of economic and political power, and capable of both planning at regional and national levels and ensuring international cooperation in defence of global environment. Historical experience of recent decades has made it abundantly clear that both the causes and consequences of, and also the solutions to, most ecological problems are national and international. Hence also the reason why, far from being incompatible, socialism and ecology presuppose one another.

At the extremes of the environmental movement, we have a certain type of ecological radicalism, which displaying its own moral absolutism with a strong focus on individual behaviour, endows all natural beings with 'rights' and pits them against humans. This 'bio-centric' view, which in a moderate form is quite widespread among ecological thinkers and activists, is much muddled and even more evasive of real issues than the mainstream environmentalism. It is muddled in ignoring that humankind, itself a natural species, even when drawing its sustenance from the rest of nature cannot be viewed as purely and simply against it, and that use of the concept of rights, itself a human invention, to downgrade humans by applying it to animals and the rest, only facilitates caricaturing of the ecological movement by its enemies. More significantly, by posing the issue as humankind versus the rest of nature, it evades and obscures the fact that the most destructive assaults upon nature come not from humanity as a whole, but from the priorities, the artefacts, and the actions of *particular* sets of human agents, whose interests are as detrimental to the majority of humankind as they are to the natural environment. The 'biocentric' view fails to recognise the real enemy of all natural beings and environment which is capitalism – very much the way it is with the mainstream environmentalism.

As I have emphasised all along, this is how the struggle for environment that began with the earth summitry in 1970, for all its thirty odd years, does not have much to show for it. A few marginal improvements have been accompanied by an overwhelming general deterioration, of which ozone depletion and global warming are only the most dramatic expressions. The conventional as well as supposedly radical solutions, stemming as they do from a misdiagnosis of the environmental crisis remain superficial and a failure, leaving environmentalism itself in a deep crisis and, as it were, at the crossroads. The differences of situation and prospects, in material or economic terms, are of course there between environmentalism of the developed North and the underdeveloped South – the 'ecologism of affluence' and the 'ecologism of survival', as one description has it. In the developed North, for obvious reasons, along with the responsibility, the possibility is greater for 'saving' or 'rehabilitating' the environment. For 'environmentalism of the poor' in the South, odds against securing sustainable development are all the greater for reasons of poverty and backwardness. But whatever the difference, the ecological movement in the South remains a poor copy of the movement in the North and the objective achievement in both cases has been negligible. Both share in the misdiagnosis of the environmental crisis and activists in both places badly need a theory capable of illuminating the necessary connections between seemingly separate problems they face and helping them understand that there are capitalist structural barriers to the effectiveness of their struggles, that, as Michel Bosquet has argued: the ecological logic is purely and simply the negation of capitalist logic; the earth cannot be saved within the framework of capitalism.

XIII

The destruction of the environment is not in any sense a natural process. It is the extensive and intensive development of the capitalist world economy that has upset the age-old patterns of balance between humanity and nature. As Foster has pointed out: 'The crisis of the earth is not a crisis of nature but a crisis of society. The chief causes of the environmental destruction that faces us today are.... social and historical, rooted in the productive relations, technological imperatives, and historically conditioned demographic trends that characterise the dominant social system.' The destruction of environment, in other words, is traceable to the forms of social production now prevalent, that is, to the grow-or-die imperatives of capitalism, its primacy of greed and predominance of economic rationality over all other forms of rationality, its market-governed structural compulsion to accumulation and unlimited growth (which, incidentally, is not the case with socialism). This destruction, and the consequent threat to the future of humankind will not be averted by the preachings and protests and partial struggles or gains of the ecologists, by better treaties and technologies or individual actions. What is required is a transformation of the social bases of environmental destruction embedded in our present-day economy. It is capitalism that has to go, superseded by a system that can ensure ecological rationality or sustainable development. Socialism with its *rationally planned* use of natural resources for human welfare is what we need, if our environment is to be saved.

This is an admittedly Marxist position. But ecologists need to turn to socialism and to Marx. The reasons are implicit, even explicit, in our argument so far. That apart, there is a specific consideration. Even if socialism is rejected, we still need to know where to go and how. And ecology simply does not have the answers. In other words, ecology by itself cannot provide a vision of the new society or a political programme of struggle for it. It has to be a part of a larger political analysis needed to move forward towards a more rational ecological and social order. Marxism, with its critique of capitalism and specifically the theory of accumulation provides a most crucial element of this larger analysis. And if capitalism is the problem, then it is logically incomplete and politically shortsighted to build a movement based primarily on ecological concerns. It needs to be remembered that 'class and exploitation' are basic to capitalist accumulation which, therefore, not only denatures and devastates the planet but also devastates and dehumanises society on a global scale. The ecological crisis is thus bound up with the other disastrous socio-economic consequence of capitalism. Capitalism today is not only unsustainable ecologically, it is also economically, politically and morally unsustainable. A programme of struggle against capitalism therefore necessarily embraces both the goal of ecological rationality and the more socially defined goals of a humane society. From the other end, ecological rationality as a critical goal is necessarily linked to others within a larger analysis and a programme of struggle for socialism. That is how to be effectively 'green', it is necessary to be 'red' as well.

Obviously a long process of theoretical clarification and learning from experience will be necessary before the ecological movement understands this, before it reaches at least that minimum degree of political consciousness which it would require to see that environment saving within capitalism is like trying to fill up a tank with almost all the taps open, before it finally understands who its real enemy is and whose interests it has to defend. The enemy is capitalism. What has to be defended against it is our very survival on this earth.

One only hopes it will not be too late. For in the meantime capitalism will have continued to ravage the environment.

XIV

The different schools of thought that have come up in contemporary 'Green Movement' – *Deep Ecology, Social Ecology, Ecofeminism, Spiritual Ecology*, etc. – have their insights and strong points, but they share, all the more because of their specific or limited focuses, in the overall limitations of mainstream environmentalism in that they either deny or tend not to acknowledge the structural bases of ecological degradation in capitalism and the class basis of effective resistance to it, or the need for a democratically organised social governance of both production and nature that is socialism. But demarcating itself sharply from and critical of Marxism is the 'ecocentric' or 'biocentric' approach, finding expression most clearly in *Deep Ecology*, which needs a brief extra comment, though I have already referred to it and will return to it later in relation to the so-called 'Prometheanism' of Karl Marx.

For 'biocentric' environmentalists, as for many others in the Green movement, socialism is irrelevant. But most of them are not friends of capitalism either. The famous green slogan, 'neither left nor right, but out front' well expresses their general position. They however push this 'out front' position to extremes as an absolute commitment to environment in which protection of environment, the 'needs of nature', take precedence over everything else, including human needs, whose satisfaction, then, can even be seen as degrading the environment. The issue is posed as 'anthropocentric' versus 'biocentric' attitude to nature. Marxism is seen as focused on human needs rather than on those of nature and thus accused of being 'anthropocentric'. It is rejected in favour of a 'biocentric' perspective in the environment movement wherein preserving nature has an intrinsic worth quite apart from any benefits this preservation may bring to present or future human generations.

This is no 'romantic primitivism', another 'back to nature' call, fashionable these days as a response to the problems of a consumerist society. Positing an absolute conflict between economic growth and environment and therefore also neglectful of political economy of environmental degradation, it is a radical insistence that intervention in nature should be guided primarily by the need to preserve biotic integrity rather than by the needs of humans. It speaks of 'restoring the natural environment and quality of life for people and other living and non-living inhabitants of the planet', thus equalising all living species and even denying any priority to the animate over the inanimate world. It would have us put 'earth first' and proposes a militant defence of 'Mother Earth' against whatever the humans may be proposing to do with it. There is a characteristic focus on the preservation of unspoiled wilderness, including opposition to dam-building in the name of 'the river's intrinsic right to remain wild'. And so on.

As a check on human arrogance and ecological hubris, its disregard for other elements in the ecosystem, the 'biocentric' view is only to be welcomed. But its underlying 'anthropocentric'—'biocentric' dichotomy is of no use in understanding the dynamics of environmental degradation. The major ecological problems facing the world today, for example, worldwide consumerism of the rich or growing militarisation with its regional wars, arms race and the prospect of nuclear annihilation, have no tangible connection to the anthropocentric – biocentric distinction. Their causes cannot be reduced to any anthropocentric attitude towards nature, and the ecological degradation they cause does not even serve the best interests of human beings. To see or understand such threats to environment in terms of anthropocentricism is at best irrelevant and at worst a dangerous obfuscation.

Again, there is a certain muddled mysticism, quasi-religiosity about biocentric view of nature. It virtually anthropomorphises nature, projects what are really human values, standards and inventions into its working, ignoring the fact that outside of human beings and their concerns, nature simply *is*; it simply has no needs, rights or purposes, no values or standards of its own. Ethics or morals belong entirely within the sphere of human potency, whatever lies outside that sphere is merely non-moral. There is no 'natural' way forward that can be 'read off' from 'Nature'. Nature exhibits no necessary harmony – much of it is 'nature, red in tooth and claw' as T.H. Huxley once described it. It is humankind that visualises harmonies, fashions moralities or introduces such things as 'laws of beauty' into nature. Notions of 'ecological balance' or 'sustainable development' make sense only in terms of human needs and purposes. Anthropocentricism alone offers a valid reference point from which to understand, evaluate and resolve ecological problems.

The biocentric approach to ecological problems is fundamentally flawed in that its anthropocentric–biocentric distinction posits a dualism between nature and society which is false. These are not in any way two diametrically opposed entities. On the contrary, nature and human society evolve, rather 'coevolve' in relation to each other as part of a complex process of mutual dependence. Humans don't stand in hostile opposition to nature but live in it and their best interests are in tune with ecological criteria. Ecological problems arise not from society's dealings with nature as such but from the *specific* ways of dealing with nature. As we have already argued, the problem lies in the current pattern of economic growth rather than in economic growth itself. Biocentric environmentalism's eco-homo dualism is not only simply false, it is also politically suicidal in the sense that it labels the human race, the people as a whole, as the enemy, obscuring the real enemy which is the historically specific economic and social order in which we live and those who hold power in it. Still worse, it has the perverse effect of strengthening the hands of these very enemies of the environment, who never tire of arguing, in the style of former American President George Bush Sr., that the environmentalists are out to take away your jobs because they care more about birds than about people.

XV

Capitalism is the real enemy. But in taking note of its inherent tendency to lay waste the environment as a consequence of its growth and accumulation imperatives, we must not underestimate 'capitalism's capacity for adaptation and its cunning', as Andre Gorz has cautioned. Capitalism has indeed shown extraordinary resilience in opposing as well accommodating the demands made on it in the name of the environment. What I have in mind here is more than its pragmatic response in terms of such things as saving on energy and reduced use of environment-harming materials, or long-term plans of 'remaking nature in ways that are consistent with sustainable profitability and capital accumulation'. Or the more recent have-your-cake-and-eat-it kind of 'free market environmentalism' where, in the aftermath of the failure of Soviet planning, pro-market economists have been claiming that capitalism can solve its own environmental problems – if only everything could be privatised and then left to 'the market'. Or 'the market incentives', 'win-win' strategies, 'green taxes' and 'ecological pricing', etc. that, World Bank down to Lester Brown of the World Watch Institute, so many have been advocating as the solution to the globe's all too many environmental problems – there is no evidence, though, that these have altered industrial production in any fundamental way. My concern here is with some aspects of capitalism's more direct engagement with environmentalism.

Typical of this engagement is the overarching fact that while defensive actions against capitalism – whether by working classes in general or by environmentalists – may curb some of its abuses, there are limits to what such actions or consequent measures can accomplish so long as the owners or agents of capital retain their positions of power. While these measures may interfere with the operations of individual capitalists, what the capitalist class cannot accept are the changes that endanger the system and its accumulation process as a whole. Long before that point is reached, the capitalist class, including the state which it controls, mobilises its defences and sets in motion counter-forces to head off and repulse the impending threat to the system. Such has been the historical experience and environment-protection measures are no exception. In other words, such measures remain, or have to remain within the systemic limits of capitalism. Again, even against such measures, capitalism is not entirely resourceless. As a rule, capital always seeks to evade any constraints on its profit-making. When it cannot defy them outright, it finds ways and means to exert control over the regulating process. It is well known how killer or polluting industries, with the support or connivance of government authorities, are eventually able to circumvent restraints on their profit-making, an activity the system respects more than saving life. When it is unable to do so, under compulsion of environmentalist pressure or government regulation, capital may simply shift the sphere of its operations within the country or move abroad, in a way producing environmental quality and safety for one group of people at the expense of the livelihood, health or lives of others. We have already noticed the marked tendency in the United States, abetted by racism, to place polluting industries and hazardous waste dumps in poor African-American, Latino, and Native American communities lacking in political power as compared to the richer and/or white neighbourhoods, and a similar worldwide tendency of global capitalism to shift dirty industries to, and dump dangerous nuclear and toxic wastes in, the poor hapless countries of the third world and, in recent years, the erstwhile second world as well.

To be specifically noted is capitalism's cooption or penetration of the mainstream environmental movement. Marcuse had drawn our attention to capitalism's capability of absorbing, repackaging, and commodifying dissent in capitalist societies. There is not much dissent here as yet, but whatever there is today stands swamped by the overwhelming presence of capitalism in the environmental movement. For even the more radical of the reformist Greens the problem is 'how to remake capitalism in ways consistent with the sustainability of nature'. Not a few in the mainstream environmentalism are trying to save capitalism from its ecologically self-destructive tendencies. Described by their critics as 'fictitious greens', they support environmental regulations consistent with profitability and the expansion of global capitalism; for example, resource conservation for long-run profitability, or profit-oriented regulation or abolition of pollution. They are, as environmental reformers, lobbyists, lawyers, or NGOs, typically allied or associated with national or international business interests, with national or multinational corporations, even as these are busy producing unhealthy, dangerous, redundant or superfluous junk, much of it designed to fall apart or become obsolete, 'to be consumed and discarded at an ever-increasing rate', so that the cycle can go on endlessly.

This, however, is only a part of the larger story of the corporate connections with or penetration of mainstream environmentalism which began much earlier but was already evident at the Rio Summit (1992). There was a large turnout of transnationals at Rio, making it a veritable meeting ground of 'penitent polluters', such as DuPont, the world's biggest producer of CFCs and now an environment protection company. The association between big business and environmentalism has grown over the years in the form of what has come to be described as the corporate 'greenwash'. In a typically significant development, even as the giant corporations go on destroying the environment and in a *jujitsu* turnaround throw the blame for it on to poorer countries, they have been making strenuous efforts to present a plausibly green image of themselves to consumers and the public. They have been busy blanketing themselves in an attractive coat of 'greenwash' which advertises them even as saviours of the environment. Joshua Karliner, in his study noted earlier, has detailed the growth of this corporate 'greenwash' which seeks to portray capitalism as the vanguard of ecological awareness. Brian Tokar, in his *Earth for Sale: Reclaiming Ecology in the Age of Corporate Greenwash,* citing a Multinational Monitor survey of the early 1990s, has pointed out that twenty-three directors and council members from several well-known environmental set-ups including the World Wildlife Fund were associated with nineteen corporations cited in the National Wildlife Federation's recent survey of the 500 worst industrial polluters, among them Union Carbide, Exxon, Monsanto, Weyerhaeuser, DuPont, and Waste Management. This apart, Du Pont is suspected of sponsoring 'Discover Underwater', Waste Management International sponsors 'Only One Earth', Gulf Oil spends more money advertising than producing 'National Geographic', and Chevron gives substantial contributions to mainstream environmental organisations such as the World Wildlife Fund, whose leaders seem to be ever eager to collaborate with greenwashing enterprise – all this to help us forget just who polluted the planet in the first place. The situation is well-expressed in the official petition for Earth Day 1995: 'With major polluters such as Texaco and Monsanto attempting to "sponsor" Earth day and every politician in the nation claiming to be "for the environment", it is getting hard to figure out who is really protecting the planet and who is polluting it.'

Capitalism can also accommodate ecological concerns in

another way, to some extent at least, by commodifying the solutions. If people will be satisfied with clean drinking water while rivers and groundwater are polluted, they will be sold bottled water or acquaguards and filters for the taps. If a biological control agent can be packaged and sold at a profit to agricultural producers, it will be. Ecological resources like soil nutrients and populations of beneficial insects can become capital stock in the market equations. In fact the problem of environmental pollution and state intervention has fitted well with the changes which have taken place in the economic basis and requirements of capitalism in recent decades. In its present form, monopoly capitalism is inclined to solve its demand problems, as we have already noticed, by extravagant expenditure at the cost of the pubic exchequer. The most obvious examples of this are unproductive investments in armaments or in space exploration. Industrial protection of the environment is emerging as a new growth area – with profit accruing to the monopolies which are often represented on state or private commissions for protection of environment in different capitalist countries. According to the calculations of the American Council of Environmental Quality at least a million dollars is pocketed in the course of the elimination of three million dollars worth of damage to the environment.

The environment industry, the production and marketing of green technologies indeed represents major business for capital and states in North America, Western Europe and Japan. Coming up in response to pressure from environmental groups and tough new regulations and enforcement, it not only helps capitalism solve its demand problems but also yields good profits. The Internal Finance Corporation (IFC) – the private lending institution of the World Bank – calculated in early 1990s that the private sector market for environmental goods and services totalled 300 billion dollars per annum, of which 100 billion was in North America and a similar amount in Europe and Japan together. Though the heady days of hazardous waste clean-up are over, the global environmental industry generated more than 400 billion dollars in revenues in 1994 and these are expected to rise to 600 billion dollars by

2010. The industry has been profitable enough to attract quite a few familiar corporate players, some with rather dubious environmental reputations. According to Larry Pratt and Wendy Montgomery, 'Mitsubishi, scourge of many of the world's greatest forests, has cornered the market on air pollution control equipment in Asia through its subsidiary, Mitsubishi Heavy Industries. In the United States, part of the environmental industry is drawn from the old military-industrial complex: corporations that once designed and manufactured weaponry for the Pentagon now work for contract on Superfund sites. Westinghouse, which once thrived on nuclear weapons contracts, now competes for Department of Energy bids to clean up the radioactive dumps the nuclear industry left behind. Several of General Electric's factories have been cited as dangerous sources of air pollution, but G.E. is now among the top manufacturers of air pollution equipment. Chemical giant DuPont, which produced some 350 million tons of waste in 1989, has developed its own toxic waste management business. The Swedish-Swiss engineering transnational, ABB Asea Brown Boveri Corp., ranked the world's third largest environmental technology company in 1995, sells coal-fired boilers to Indonesia, already coping with serious air pollution, because the US utilities market has dropped due to a shift to low-sulphur coal.' And so on.

Increasingly, the demand for environmental technologies and services is coming from the so-called 'emerging markets' of Asia, Latin America and East Europe. Coming up in the 1980s, the environment industries entered the era of globalisation nineties onward, especially after the advent of the World Trade Organisation, moving to China, India, South Korea, Mexico, Brazil, Poland, the Czech Republic with the strong support of their home countries and multilateral development banks – and in some cases, of large and influential non-governmental organisations (NGOs), which, incidentally, again raises the question whether they are promoting the cause of transnational ecology or of transnational capital. It has been and remains a struggle among the advanced industrial countries over share in the global environmental market. As for those at the receiving end of this struggle, this is what Pratt and Montgomery have to say: 'The growing involvement of the oligopolistic environmental industry in the ecological affairs of developing countries – at least those countries that can attract its investment – offers little more than the greening of global reach, a new colouration of the same old imperialism'.

The environment industry, it should be noted, deals with ecological problems only *ex post facto*, that is after the damage has been done. And it is a damage done by straightforward industry itself. In other words, firms in the environmental technologies industry are involved in cleaning up the hazardous wastes, controlling the pollution, repairing the damage which, as resource producers, chemical manufacturers and utilities, they themselves or their kin have created. Capitalism thus makes profits both ways, while degrading the environment as also while trying to save it. It makes profits on the straightforward market where consumer goods for private consumption are produced with increasing ecological degradation and then where the same degradation has to be contained by the use of environmental technologies. In the latter case the profits are made with a clear conscience as well.

Money and conscience-wise it is as good as it can be for capitalism. But it has not worked for environment. Capitalism's 'capacity for adaptation and its cunning', here and for that matter elsewhere, may have ameliorated some environmental problems, but this has hardly made any difference in global terms. The ensemble of environmental problems that is the global ecological crisis remains and grows daily more complex. Radical changes are called for, but little is accomplished within the system and the problem only intensifies. Which however is not surprising. For it is system itself, the very *nature* of production for the market which is the problem. Paul Hawken, well-known 'mail-order catalogue impresario' who surely knows his 'over-consuming' Americans, has thus recognised the real situation: 'Despite their dedicated good work, if we examine all or any of the businesses that deservedly earn high marks for social and environmental responsibility, we are faced with a sobering irony: If every company on the planet were to adopt the environmental and social practices of the best companies – of, say, the Body Shop, Patagonia, and Ben and Jerry's – the world would still be moving toward environmental degradation and collapse. In other words, if we analyse environmental effects and create an input-output model of resources and energy, the results do not even approximate a tolerable or sustainable future. If a tiny fraction of the world's most intelligent companies cannot model a sustainable world, then that tells us that .... what we have is not a management problem but a design problem.'

'A design problem' – it could not have been put better. It is indeed the design or structural logic of capitalist market economy – an economy driven by competition and endless pursuit of profit, and therefore given to overproduction and 'over-consumption' – which lies behind the continued degradation of the environment, and makes 'a sustainable world' impossible. That is how, despite the development of a growing environmental consciousness and the movements to which it has given rise in recent decades, the environmental crisis continues to deepen. There is nothing in the record or on the horizon that could lead us to believe that any significant change for the better is likely in the future within capitalism.

XVI

It is our argument then that the environmental crisis is, at its core, a crisis of capitalism. It is a function of its inherent nature as an uncontrolled process of profit-making and capital accumulation, of the characteristically capitalist commitment to growth and expansion at any cost, reinforced by, and increasingly inseparable from, consumerism and, it should be added, a pervasive, technologically sophisticated military machine, which is a major and potentially catastrophic polluter in its own right. The system contains no braking mechanism other than periodic economic breakdowns. In its normal functioning, the individual units of which it is composed – the separate capitals – must respond to relatively short-run profit prospects on pain of elimination; nothing else counts, least of all natural environment. In its latest phase, after its consumerist profligacy, armament industries and wars, and universal wastefulness, the destructive potential of capitalism has acquired a new quality in the form of an 'ecological crisis', entailing irreversible damage to the environment. A fundamental change has occurred in the relationship between human beings and the environment. Human actions that in the past merely produced local environmental problems now have, in their cumulative outcome, most dangerous global implications. Capitalism has brought humankind at a turning point in its history.

Destruction of the ozone layer, the greenhouse effect, heat waves and global warming, climatic changes with droughts, floods and famines in tow, annihilation of ancient and tropical forests, species extinction, loss in genetic diversity, production of radio-active and toxic wastes, contamination of water resources, soil erosion, depletion of essential natural resources, desertification, the growth of world population spurred by rising poverty – all this and more represent ominous trends which portend incalculable loss in human lives, eco systems and entire cultures, the ultimate destruction of human habitat itself.

The sustainability of both human civilisation and global life processes depends not on the mere slowing down of these dire trends, but on their *reversal*. Nothing in the past or the present of capitalism however suggests that the system will be up to such a task. It is a task which requires a system organised on very different principles, with different priorities and answering to different needs, where the maximisation of private profit is not the dominant principle, capitalist control over economy is replaced with control by and for the people, and economic growth is guided and controlled, even curtailed if necessary, to confront the present ecological crisis and the long-term issues of sustainable development. Principles, priorities and needs which govern capitalism are inherently ill-suited to confronting today's ecological crisis or ensuring sustainable development. On the contrary, there is every indication that the system, left to its own devices, will gravitate towards the 'let them eat pollution' stance as *The Economist* phrased it. There is nothing in the system that lends itself to or is compatible with long-range planning of a kind that would be absolutely essential to securing a reversal of the present trends and implementation of an effective ecological programme. It is precisely in this respect that socialism as an economic system represents a decisive break with capitalism. One of the central ideas of socialism has always been the substitution of planning for the market as the overall allocator of resources. In the capitalist market, the pursuit and maximisation of profit is the decisive consideration, the driving force behind the accumulation of *private* capital. Under socialism, profit can and may serve as a criterion of viability and accounting but does not have to be maximised. What is to be maximised is social good and accumulation of *public* capital for the same purpose. Socialism is a way of organising the social production and distribution of goods and services to respond to the needs of the population. Based on the collective ownership of the means of production (whose forms can be varied) and planning, it can allocate resources for achieving the desired results, and one, right at the top, can be the protection and preservation of the environment, or it ought to be. In other words, socialism is today a necessary, though by no means sufficient, condition for saving the environment and living in harmony with it, for ensuring a sustainable economic development in the interests of the people.

XVII

The above argument, so sound, rational and plausible, is in effect a restatement of the traditional Marxist case for socialism. Socialism meant the triumph of an elementary kind of rationality, a democratically planned use of human and natural resources for the benefit of humankind, which would almost axiomatically preclude the kind of environmental destruction that capitalism has entailed and which, if persisted in, would mean the suicide of the human species. The underlying assumption was, and still is, that socialism will not only reverse the process of environmental destruction inherited from centuries of capitalism and repair the damage, but also obviate the very possibility of any kind of ecological crisis or disaster that we face today.

However self-evident or persuasive once, with more than 70 years of 'socialist' history behind us, the argument has seemingly lost all credibility, raising a whole lot of controversial issues regarding socialism, and beyond that even Marxism itself. People don't see the connections between capitalism and environmental crisis, and Marxism cannot make any special claims to be friendly to environment – at the very least Marx is seen to have failed to incorporate ecological concerns into his socialist project. For, so far as environment is concerned, the record of socialism as practised in the Soviet Union and Eastern Europe has on the whole been no better than that of capitalism. Given the prevalent equation of socialism as such with its first historical manifestation in these countries, many have seen an inherent similarity between capitalism and socialism and distanced themselves from any sharply focussed anti-capitalism. Capitalism per se is not the culprit, it is argued, nor socialism an answer to the environmental crisis.

The ecological performance of the communist regimes in the Soviet Union and East Europe has indeed been dismal, though their very economic failures – which were a part of their economic successes – set some limits on the damage done. The evidence is there in the filthy waters of Volga, the pollution of Lake Baikal and the polluted air of Don Basin, the destruction of the Aral Sea and salt deserts of Central Asia, 80 per cent dead or dying forests of what was once Czechoslovakia, and so on. Pointing out that environmental problems are not limited to the capitalist countries, Barry Commoner has written: 'By far the worst cases of radioactive contamination, of which the accident at Chernobyl is only the most spectacular, have occurred in the Soviet Union; Czechoslovakia and Poland have the highest levels of industrial pollutants in Europe, and perhaps the world; the socialist countries, especially the Soviet Union, have rapidly adopted the same agricultural chemicals that are responsible for polluted water supplies and pesticide-contaminated food in the United States and Europe....' This obviously raises the question of why these regimes, which claimed to be socialist went so wrong ecologically. The answer, if a trifle less obvious, lies in the deformed character of what they built there as socialism – 'actually existing socialism' we have called it – though we still need to know why and how they went wrong.

It needs to be clearly understood that the environmental failure of the communist regimes, unlike capitalism, is not traceable to anything structurally inherent in socialism as a mode of economic production, nor does it indicate any inherent powerlessness of socialist planning to cope with environmental problems. It was essentially a human failure, rather the failure of their leadership as socialists. In capitalism, it should be noted, ecological damage is less an index of failure than a mask of success of capitalism, a working out of its structural logic; it is not a departure from capitalist principles but, on the contrary, their inevitable by-product, a response to the imperatives of profit-making and capital accumulation. More successful capitalism is, more damage it does to environment. Against this socialism understood in classical Marxist terms has no such logic or imperative. Put simply, it is a system of planned production governed by the direct producers and aimed at use, not profit or capital accumulation. The environmental destruction in the communist regimes, therefore, was indeed a failure, but a failure caused not by socialism but, on the contrary by a *deficit* of socialist values and practices, that is by a departure from socialist principles.

Underlying this departure from socialist principles are the historical conditions governing the construction of socialism in the Soviet Union and a specific theoretical *deficit* – the minor economistic tendency or 'productivist bias' within classical Marxism which thanks to these conditions, acquired a new lease of life to become, as 'economism', a dangerously effective deforming influence on what ultimately got constructed there. I will return to the question of 'productivist bias' in Marxism later in these notes. Immediately I would like to note – as we have done in other contexts – the historical conditions of the socialist experiment in the Soviet Union, the way they made for the ascendancy of 'economism' in this experiment with obviously damaging consequences for the environment.

The environmental failure in the Soviet Union was above

all a historical product – result of the global context in which the first effort to build socialism was made – not only in a relatively underdeveloped country but against the fanatical resistance and hostility of the more powerful capitalist countries. Soviet planning, from the outset till the very end, had to focus on goals perceived (rightly in the opinion of discerning critics) as being matters of immediate survival. This meant an exclusive concern throughout with defence preparedness and with economic growth at all costs to 'catch up' with western industrial development in the shortest possible time. Given this exclusive concern, 'economism' took over the construction of socialism, the speediest possible overtaking of the leading capitalist countries was seen as the principal task of socialist strategy, and such overtaking, say in per capita pig iron, steel or coal production, became the measure of socialist success. Soviet Union's 'socialist production and accumulation', as it was called, was indeed a remarkable achievement but it meant the subordination and ultimate disappearance of other socialist goals such as equality, the liberation of women, a humane work environment, the creation of a cooperative, egalitarian, democratic and ultimately classless society. Economic growth and defence preparedness taking precedence over everything else, the state was reinforced and more than ever centralised in the form of the Party-State, instead of embarking on the road to its 'withering away', as envisaged in the original socialist project. The crucial preoccupations of Marxism were reduced to a liturgy used on rare festive occasions.

Economism and not revolutionary socialist politics governing its socialist project, Soviet Union invented a new way of extracting surplus but not any different patterns of production and consumption. It competed with capitalism not in terms of socialist principles or values, but on the latter's own terrain – the terrain of economic growth. As a result the socialist project in the Soviet Union was never able to distance itself from capitalist criteria of success or its structures and methods. These were taken for granted as directly usable – a good example is the most intensive exploitative practices of *Taylorism* to force a high rate of surplus-labour extraction from the workers. Such emulation of capitalism or borrowing from it naturally reproduced many of the worst evils and excesses of capitalism including wanton neglect and abuse of the environment. The environmental depredations of the hitherto existing socialism are thus clearly traceable to its capitalist context, its susceptibility to capitalist drives and pressures both internally and externally. The inherited habits of private ambition, hierarchy, and repression only solidified under conditions of military and economic encirclement, and the technology, the emphasis on reckless growth, and the fear of 'falling behind', that came directly from the surrounding industrialised capitalist countries, pushed the production system further into acquiring some of the worst features of capitalism, notwithstanding the people's idealist inspiration of early years to build socialism as a different kind of society.

It is not that concern for environment was always lacking in the revolutionary leadership or the Soviet state and society. According to John Bellamy Foster, Soviet ecology in the 1920s was arguably the most advanced in the world because, as he says, Soviet thinking was more dynamic, dialectically complex, holistic and coevolutionary while the western models tended to be reductionist, linear and teleological. He has cited Vernadsky's analysis of the biosphere and Vavilov's work on genetic diversity, as well as Lenin's and Lunacharsky's policies of environmental protection. Bukharin's writings, particularly his recently published *Philosophical Arabesques*, show him to be a deep ecological thinker. The Soviet state had passed some of the most advanced environmental protection laws in the world. But concerns of early revolutionary leaders were soon overtaken by the principles of what amounted to a war economy and as 'economism' took over, the environmental protection laws were in practice disregarded and unenforced. Things really took a bad turn after the ascendancy of Stalin and the first five-year plan, when conservation was attacked as 'bourgeois' and when the more ecological thinkers were purged.

If 'economism' of the earlier period had witnessed the adoption of capitalist principles and methods of production in the name of the revolution and for the declared purpose of the necessary 'socialist accumulation', the rather depoliticised 'economism' of the latter years opted for them in the name of a so-called 'scientific management' of economy and society – in both cases regardless of the environmental consequences. It has been pointed out that most of the systems of production that the 'socialist' countries adopted during this latter period were in fact developed in the capitalist countries after World War II – for example, chemical agriculture, nuclear power plants, and the petrochemical industry. And as a scholar has commented: 'Having been developed with no concern for their environmental impact, these production systems wreak their havoc on the environment equally in capitalist countries and the socialist ones. It is, after all, unreasonable to expect that the automobiles produced in the Soviet Union at Togliattigard, by a plant imported intact from the Italian company, Fiat, would refrain from emitting the same pollutants in Moscow that they produce in Rome – perhaps out of respect for socialism.'

One may add that if the emphasis on survival did not allow the societies of 'actually existing socialism' the resources or the possibility to direct attention to preservation of the environment in the earlier period, the new ruling classes, as they grew up there, probably were not inclined to do that in any case, any more than the ruling classes in the capitalist societies. The absence of democracy in the state and the party only ensured that the advocates of social interests such as environmentalism were never free to comment on or criticise, let alone influence, government decisions – as, incidentally, they are able to, to an extent, in democratic capitalist societies, where, however limited they may be, the positive achievements of environmentalism reflect organised resistance to market pressure, with market mechanisms themselves sometimes transmitting such resistance by the people, as, for example, when they decide to stay away from or boycott polluted or polluting products.

Thus, it has been argued that the historical conditions of the first existence of socialism – extreme economic backwardness and implacably hostile capitalist encirclement – gave a strong economistic or productivist bias to its construction. Economic backwardness has its own compulsions to develop forces of production to overcome it. Despite the possibility of some improvement with limited resources, the simple fact remains that the poverty and misery of millions of people cannot be overcome without major advances in agricultural output, industrialisation, labour productivity and the application of advanced science and technology. But global capitalism's threat to its very survival, throughout its 70 years long existence, turned this bias into a mania for economic growth and gigantism in its planning; ever expanding growth, economically and militarily, became the overriding consideration. The planning process lost its vision of socialism – which is primarily about changing social relations of production to create a fraternal and egalitarian society and not just developing the forces of production – and its implementers their ability to recognise discrepancies between what they were doing and what they ought to or might have done. Production for production's sake (rather than production for use) seemed to have replaced production for profit. Although the logic of accumulation in the 'actually existing socialism' of Soviet Union or Eastern Europe differed markedly from that of capitalism – governed as it was not by compulsions of the market but by political decisions whatever their quality may have been – the direction of their productive activity largely came to resemble the patterns of capitalist development. Under these circumstances, the impact of 'actually existing socialism' on the environment also came to be hardly distinguishable from that of capitalism.

XVIII

In a fundamental sense that goes beyond this explanation of what went wrong – and the viability of this explanation cannot be denied – the environmental failure of 'actually existing socialism', as part of its general failure, is traceable to serious inadequacies of theory and political practice in coping with the unprecedented and entirely unanticipated task – so far as classical Marxist perspective is concerned – of having to build socialism and that too for the first time, in a poor backward country, and in a world dominated by global capitalism. And it has to be conceded that while some of these inadequacies were born of 'silences' or 'empty spaces' in Marxism, others are traceable to certain mistaken tendencies that had already grown within Marxism in the course of its historical development. Particularly noticeable in the immediate context is 'economism' or 'productivist bias' in Marxism – we have previously noticed it on more than one occasion (for example, in relation to Marxism of the Second International) – which virtually grew into 'a theory of productive forces' in the Soviet socialist construction.

This productivist bias or thrust in classical Marxism, a minor tendency within it which acquired a dangerous pre-eminence only due to historical circumstances both before and after the October Revolution, is not difficult to understand. It has been suggested that as a product of its time Marxism's break with the productivist pattern of industrial capitalism and with the foundations of the modern bourgeois civilisation was not sufficiently radical. Be that as it may, Marxism, in its own way, shared in the prevalent ideology of progress, the hopeful ethos and scientific-technological optimism of the nineteenth century, which saw the development of the productive forces as the very basis of all material progress and therefore by its nature something positive. This productivist orientation got reinforced by Marxism's understanding of capitalism and its future and the origins and purpose of socialism as a mode of production which transcends it. Even as capitalism was subjected to a remarkably perceptive empirical and ethical critique and its transitory nature underlined, capitalism was seen as playing a *progressive* historical role in that it creates the objective, material basis for socialism by its development of the forces of production. As Marx put it: 'Development of the productive forces of social labour is the historical task and justification of capital. This is the way it unconsciously creates the requirements of a higher mode of production.' This higher mode of production, socialism, takes over and indeed legitimises itself by accelerating the development of forces of production to the point where scarcity is overcome and the transition to a realm of abundance – not in any absolute sense but in terms of satisfaction of basic material needs of all – becomes a historical possibility, providing the conditions for a future of real human emancipation, which for Marx lies beyond the realm of material production, in the working out of our truly human creative powers, as he clearly stated it in his *Economic and Philosophic Manuscript of 1844*, and later works such as the *Grundrisse, Capital* and *Critique of the Gotha Programme*.

A particular reinforcement for the productivist bias came from the radical political thrust of Marxism. Since the days when Aristotle argued in defence of slavery as a prerequisite of 'good life' for a few, such and similar arguments, invoking 'natural limits' have been regularly deployed to deny the possibility of decent human living for every one and justify the inequalities and iniquities of the prevalent social orders. Marxism rejected, as necessarily conservative, all such foreclosing of human possibilities on this earth. It set no limits to natural resources at the disposal of humankind and was optimistic that science and technology, together with human knowledge and capabilities will take care of any problems that may arise. Scholars have seen this productivist bias reinforced in another way too, by Marxism's traditional and quite proper concern with impoverishment and deprivation in society, so that the liberation or development of the productive forces came to be viewed as the privileged and to some degree exclusive means towards a better life and the broader goal of human emancipation.

Productivism thus indeed found a niche in Marxism. But classical Marxism as such was never productivist. Far from being any kind of believers in productivism, Marx and Engels were two of its foremost critics. This is what the young Engels wrote in 1844: 'To make the earth an object of huckstering – the earth which is our one and all, the first condition of our existence – was the last step toward making oneself an object of huckstering'. About the same time, in one of his earliest writings, this is how Marx expressed himself on the subject: 'In the development of productive forces there comes a stage when productive forces and means of intercourse are brought into being which under the existing relations only cause mischief, and are no longer productive but destructive forces .... These productive forces achieve under the system of private property a one-sided development only, and for the majority they become destructive forces. Thus things have now come to such a pass that the individuals must appropriate the existing totality of productive forces, not only to achieve self-activity, but, also, merely to safeguard their very existence.'

When Engels warned or Marx wrote these lines, in 1844, the 'one-sidedly developed productive/destructive forces' identified by them were still very far from being fully developed, as they are now – some of them even acquiring an autonomous destructive character of their own. They underline the possibility of 'the total destruction of humanity' that Marx warned of as a result of capital's unrestrainable drive for self-expansion and accumulation. Marx indeed visualised this possibility, but never gave much thought to its becoming a reality. Giving capitalism a short lease of life, he never seriously considered that its 'development of productive forces' can one day endanger human survival by threatening to destroy the natural environment.

Marx's rejection of 'productivism' is most clearly evident in the few observations he made in his early writings, or was later provoked to make by the flawed thinking of his disciples in Germany, about the communist society of the future. Marx saw capitalism as a society of multiple alienations. Private property, class relations, wage labour, and the fetishisms of market exchange separate and alienate us from any sensuous and immediate contact (except in the fragmented and partial sense achievable under class-ordered divisions of labour) with 'nature' as they alienate us from other human beings. We stand alienated even from ourselves, our *species-being*. All natural and human relationship are dissolved into money relationships. Rather than a society sick with alienation and ruled by 'callous cash-payment' and by the necessity for continual increases in productivity, Marx looked forward to a social order that would promote the many-sided development of human capacities and a rational human relation to nature which, as he wrote in the final part of the third volume of *Capital*, consists in 'socialised man, the associated producers, rationally regulating their material interchange with nature.... with the least expenditure of energy and under conditions most favourable to, and worthy of, their human nature'. This rational control of the relation between nature and humanity is inherently opposed to the mechanistic domination of nature in the interest of the ever increasing expansion of production for its own sake. In a society of freely associated producers, Marx argued, the goal of social life would not be work and production, in the narrow forms in which they have been understood in possessive-individualist society of capitalism, but the all-around development of human creative potential, for which, he further argued, 'the shortening of the working-day is a basic prerequisite'. This would set the stage for what Marx spoke of as 'the realm of freedom... beyond the sphere of actual material production (where) begins that development of human power which is an end in itself'.

Productivism thus is no integral part of Marxism. As 'productivist bias' it was only a minor tendency within classical Marxism. But given this tendency, it is not difficult to understand that, under compulsion of historical circumstances or pressure, it should take the form of a vulgar Marxism where the aim of social revolution is not a fraternal and egalitarian reorganisation of society, not a social order with a new way of producing and living, with production relations and indeed productive forces of a qualitatively different nature, but simply the abolition of capitalist ownership or control of production as obstacles to the free development of productive forces, and then the further development of these forces. Something like this is indeed what happened with 'actually existing socialism' – the development of productive forces became the decisive concern which overshadowed everything else and pushed the socialist vision into complete oblivion. The destruction of environment was one consequence. There was other, even more disastrous, as we now know. The effort to build socialism itself ended in an ignominious collapse.

The most important implication of the above argument is that there was nothing inevitable about what has happened. Marxism can and must do without productivist bias and socialism does not have to necessarily yield to it and lose its 'utopian' vision. It may not be of much use to now speculate whether, given a different global context in which they felt secure and were able to purse their own goals free of outside pressure, the societies of 'actually existing socialism' would have fared and built better; though it cannot be ruled out that given more adequate Marxist theory and better political leadership, even in the global context that was theirs, they could have fared and built better and could have had a qualitatively different impact on the environment. But on the basis of their experience, it can certainly be argued that socialism or socialist planning is not necessarily environmentally destructive and that it was so in these societies because it never transcended the capitalist context from which it had emerged. If and when a socialist society of the future is able to reorder its priorities from 'catching up' and defence to protection and preservation of the environment – seen as the life-and-death issue they are rapidly becoming – it certainly cannot be excluded in advance that its planning system can well achieve these new goals.

Argument here is *not* that socialism will automatically go on to deal successfully with the threat of ecological disaster that has been inherited from centuries of capitalism, or that it guarantees that none of its other immediate or long term goals will obstruct ecological wisdom. But in practically eliminating the market-based vested economic interests which perpetuate ecologically harmful practices, it does acquire the potential of making significant advances towards ecologically rational production. A socialist framework has certainly facilitated Cuba's recent turn to an eco-friendly, pesticide-free development just as Nicaragua under Sandinista leadership had made notable progress towards freeing itself of pesticide dependence. Particularly in countries of the third world which, subject to imperialist domination or pressure, are suffering capitalism's most severe environmental abuses, any successful move away from capitalism certainly offers great scope for improvement. The argument, then, is that a socialist planning is not necessarily powerless to cope with environmental problems. At the very least, unlike capitalism, socialism offers the *possibility* of coping with them successfully.

Socialism, needless to say, is not any one's utopia. Even if it finds its real democratic form, it is bound to do many things badly, and for a long-time, in some cases do even more badly than capitalism. The relevant questions, however, are whether it has decisively broken with, and once and for all stopped emulating capitalism, whether it has set itself the right goals and is genuinely striving to achieve them. If and when these questions can be answered in the affirmative we shall be on the road to salvation not only environment-wise but in much else besides. It is thus that humankind under threat, in its search for survival may yet discover socialism as a viable form of humane society, a real alternative to consumerism-ridden capitalism.

Despite all the failures and disappointments of its first experiment, socialism remains the only possible framework for reversing the looming ecological breakdown. I will only add that as the consequences of such a breakdown become clear and are seen to be inescapable within capitalism, we may yet, for this reason alone, see a revival of interest in socialism before long.

XIX

Its nineteenth-century origins or sharing in the ethos of the times drunk on the achievements of science and technology notwithstanding, there is no 'hostility' to nature or productivist triumphalism in classical Marxism. Critics however continue to accuse it of being anti-ecological, of an essentially anti-nature 'Prometheanism' as they call it. Minor aspects or odd statements are taken out of context or superficially interpreted in an effort to find a 'smoking gun' to demonstrate that Marx and Engels adopted a one-sided, exploitative view of nature. Thus critics have regularly pointed to a passage by Engels in *Anti-Duhring* on the growing mastery of nature that will ensue once human beings have transcended social alienation: 'The seizure of the means of production by society puts an end to commodity production, and therewith to the domination of the product over the producer. Anarchy in social production is replaced by conscious organisation on a planned basis. The struggle for individual existence comes to an end. And at this point, in a certain sense, man finally cuts himself off from the animal world, leaves the conditions of animal existence behind him and entres conditions which are really human. The conditions of existence forming man's environment, which up to now have dominated man, at this point pass under the dominion and control of man, who now for the first time becomes the real conscious master of Nature, because and in so far as he has become master of his own social organisation. The laws of his own social activity, which have hitherto confronted him as external, dominating laws of Nature, will then be applied by man with complete understanding, and hence will be dominated by man. Men's own social organisation which has hitherto stood in opposition to them as if arbitrarily decreed by Nature and history, will then become the voluntary act of men themselves. The objective, external forces which have hitherto dominated history, will then pass under the control of men themselves. It is only from this point that men, with full consciousness, will fashion their own history; it is only from this point that the social causes set in motion by men will have, predominantly and in constantly increasing measure, the effects willed by men. It is humanity's leap from the realm of necessity into the realism of freedom.' Even a sympathetic scholar like Ted Benton has criticised Engels on the grounds that such a view 'presupposes control over nature' and hence 'an underlying antagonism between human purposes and nature: either we control nature, or it controls us'. In other words Engels is said to have adopted an extreme anthropocentric rather than ecocentric perspective.

At times even the entire argument of a writing is misinterpreted as evidence of Marx's pro-technological and anti-ecological productivist orientation. Thus *Communist Manifesto* has been viewed by critics as a work that is wholly productivist in character and steeped in notions of progress and the subjection of nature that are deeply anti-nature. It is taken to be entirely oblivious to environmental concerns. There is the typical post-modernist criticism too which sees Marxism as one of the main means by which the Baconian notion of the mastery of nature was transmitted to the modern world. Even as she recognises that 'Marx and Engels displayed an extraordinary understanding of and sensitivity toward the "ecological" costs of capitalism', socialist ecofeminist Carolyn Merchant yet writes: '....they nevertheless bought into the Englightenment's myth of progress via the domination of nature.' It is indeed common for critics to argue that it is not only those claiming to be their followers who have treated nature as an object to be exploited – which is certainly true of many of them – but that, notwithstanding the ecological sensitivity they displayed in particular areas, the world view of Marx and Engels themselves was rooted in the notion of technological subjection of nature by man. Ecologists have seen this as a basic flaw in Marxism. Marx has been charged with 'Prometheanism', and in their eco-centrism, the ecologists have so emphasised its supposed 'anti-naturalism' that we hear of 'much bad blood between Marxists and ecologists'.

Marxism has also been charged with insufficient recognition of the limits that nature imposes on the development of humanity, or of inter-generational responsibilities that Otto Neurath and others have recently argued for. Ted Benton has argued that Marx 'exaggerate(s) the potentially transformative character (of productive labour processes) whilst under-theorising or occluding the various respects in which they are subject to naturally given and/or relatively non-manipulable conditions and limits', and claimed that Marx had become a victim of a spontaneous ideology of the nineteenth century, namely, industrialism and progress. This criticism has been in many ways reinforced on the one hand by the terrible ecological record of 'actually existing socialism', confused with socialism *as such*, and by the overwhelming gravity of the environmental crisis on the other.

In assessing such criticism which, on textual or other grounds, faults Marx and Engels on ecological issues, it helps to remember the historical context of their work and writings. They lived and wrote at a time when most thinkers saw nature and human beings as diametrically opposed to one another and science was seen as not only allowing humanity to escape nature's dominance and to become dominant in turn, but also finding nature bountiful. Words like 'mastery', 'domination', 'conquest', or 'subjection' of nature as well as 'bountiful nature' were part of the dominant discourse on the subject. Again, the environmental question did not find a great deal of attention in Marx's time because, though nascent industrialists were already wreaking havoc on the environment, their impact was still limited and localised. Marx and Engels' own critique of capitalism's accumulation process, beginning with their very earliest writings, indeed led them to conclude that the system lacked a sustainable relation to nature. In their analysis, however, this problem did not yet loom so large that it would affect the future of capitalism (which they thought was in any case destined to die soon as a result of its economic and political contradictions). It was, so to speak, not *their* problem. They were indeed aware of the destructive nature of capitalist 'interchange with nature' and even concerned about it. But giving capitalism only a short lease of life, they could not be too concerned about how destructive it would ultimately turn out to be. If the issue of ecological sustainability was nevertheless raised in their works, it was part of their critique of capitalism and had still more to do with their understanding of the needs of the future society of freely associated producers. Marx wanted to make it very clear that the stability of any future society would be dependent on the creation of a wholly new and more balanced, 'non-alienated' relation to the natural world.

Even so, critics have been rather superficial in their understanding or interpretation of the textual evidence. Marx's approach to environmental issues in the *Communist Manifesto*, for example, is obviously inadequate if viewed by itself; but it is not so if the context, that is, the nature of the document is kept in mind. As Foster has pointed out: 'The *Manifesto* was first and foremost a revolutionary document, but ecological contradictions, though perceived by Marx and Engels even at this early stage in their analysis, play little or no role in the anticipated revolution against capitalism. Marx and Engels clearly thought that the duration of capitalism would be much shorter than earlier modes of production, brought to a relatively rapid end by the intensity of its contradictions and by the actions of the proletariat – the gravedigger of the system. As a result, they tended to view the ecological problems that they perceived as having more bearing on the future of communist than capitalist society. This is why ecological considerations enter much more explicitly into their programme for communism in the *Manifesto* than into their assessment of the conditions leading to the demise of capitalism.'

Again, apropos that often quoted passage from *Anti-Duhring*, Foster writes: 'But is Engels' argument here really vulnerable to such criticism? Despite the use of such terms as "master of Nature" the intent of this passage ought to be quite clear. It is that a revolution in social organisation is necessary to allow human beings to avoid being simply prey to natural forces (or forces that purport to be "natural", as capitalist economic forces are represented in bourgeois political economy). In fact, what is being celebrated here is not human mastery of nature so much as the human mastery of the making of history, which gives humanity the capacity to reorganise its relation to nature, under conditions of human freedom and the full development of human needs and potentials. There is nothing here to suggest an underlying antagonism towards nature in Engels' notion of the realm of freedom. Communism, Engels observed elsewhere, was a society in which people would "not only feel, but also know, their *unity* with nature".' It may be added that 'the domination of nature' was seen by Marx and Engels as a phase of historical development – part and parcel of the whole self-alienation of human society, which also meant its alienation from nature – which would be transcended under communism.

Details of critics' argument, their particular misunderstandings of Marx need not detain us. More important is to note the fact of their overall underestimation of Marx's achievement, the rich legacy of his thought on ecological issues. No doubt, as in case of so much else outside the realm of economy proper, here too we do not have a comprehensive or theorised statement by him, but the space here is not entirely empty either. What is significant and a mark of his genius is the way he transcends the nineteenth century even as he belonged to it. This is evident in his scattered insights and statements, in whatever little he said on ecological issues. And scholars have not been entirely wanting in recognising this. Massimo Quaini has noted that Marx 'denounced the spoliation of nature before a modern bourgeois ecological conscience was born'; William Leiss in his pioneering study *The Domination of Nature*, concludes that taken together, the writings of Marx and Engels 'represent the most profound insight into the complex issues surrounding the mastery of nature to be found anywhere in nineteenth century thought or *a fortiori* in the contributions of earlier periods'. And as Foster has put it: 'No other thinker in Marx's time, and perhaps no other thinker up to our own day, has so brilliantly captured the full complexity of the relationship between nature and modern society'. It is indeed remarkable how, without any pretensions to finished or final answers, Marx addresses the more basic issues of ecology today and provides insights into problems of our living at the beginning of the twenty-first century.

Marx had, well ahead of most contemporary environmental thought, already in the nineteenth century posed many of the essential ecological questions that are our concern today: questions regarding the overall relation between nature and human society, the inter-dependent 'metabolic' character of the evolving human-nature interaction, the connection between the exploitation of the earth and other forms of exploitation, and above all the question of sustainability. It is not surprising therefore that recent years have witnessed new interest in Marx's ecological thought and there has been much scholarly writing on the subject. Particularly noteworthy here is the pioneering work of John Bellamy Foster. His new book, *Marx's Ecology: Materialism and Nature*, is arguably the most outstanding writing on the subject so far, bringing together as it does the ideas and insights of Marx and Engels as a part of their philosophy as a whole, in a framework of environmental history based on a historical-materialist approach. It is not possible nor necessary to share this or other recent explorations of Marx's ecology in these notes. I will only try to convey something of the flavour of Marx and Engels' ecological thinking with the help of a few quotes from their own writings.

Marx refers to nature as 'man's inorganic body' and to man as 'a part of nature'. As he wrote in the *Economic and Philosophic Manuscripts of 1844*: 'Man lives from nature, i.e., nature is his body, and he must maintain a continuing dialogue with it if he is not to die. To say that man's physical and mental life is linked to nature simply means that nature is linked to itself, for man is a part of nature'. This doesn't simply mean that humans cannot free themselves from the need to take into consideration the natural conditions of human existence. That 'man lives from nature, i.e., nature is his body' also implies that the health of that body is fundamental to man's own health; to respect nature is to respect ourselves. This insistence on the natural basis of human production, its dependence on natural conditions and the need to take good care of these conditions, does not however indicate what Burkett has called a 'crudely naturist' approach that many ecologists seem to propose, some kind of going back to a 'face to face', unmediated relation to nature. For Marx all human production is socially mediated production and occurs within a co-evolutionary context. The notion of co-evolution of nature and humanity is central to Marx's understanding of the relation between the two. Human development, the unfolding of human potentials and the emergence of new needs and talents presupposes the material production and reproduction of life and of means of subsistence, processes through which both humans and nature change, and change each other. As human beings engage in production and transform nature, they also transform themselves, though, it must be added, human production and the accompanying self-transformation can only partially transcend their natural bases. Human freedom and self-transformation (or self-creation as it can also be called) is a reality but it is circumscribed in that it does not exist independently or in defiance of natural conditions and natural laws.

Marx, even as he recognised that humanity and nature are necessarily interrelated in a process of coevolutionary 'social metabolism', also pointed out that it is the historically specific form of social production relations which constitutes the core of that interrelationship in any given period and that in the modern period, capitalist production relations have meant a near total alienation of not only social but natural conditions of human existence as well. Human beings stand alienated from nature too. For Marx, it is this which must be at the centre of our attention. 'It is not the unity of living and active humanity with the natural, inorganic conditions of their metabolic exchange with nature, and hence their appropriation of nature,' Marx wrote, 'which requires explanation or is the result of a historic process, but rather the separation between these inorganic conditions of human existence and this active existence, a separation which is completely posited only in the relation of wage labour and capital.' It is this realistic approach which explains Marx's dealing with the ecological issues not as an independent question, or in the abstract, but in relation to his critique of capitalism and vision of the future communist society.

For Marx, material wealth in its widest conception (understood in terms of use values) has to be distinguished from value creation under capitalism (the world of exchange value). Genuine wealth, for him, consists of use values which are produced only with the help of nature. Nature is one of the sources in the creation of wealth, along with labour or labour power. Marx wrote that 'labour is the natural condition of the human, the condition of material exchange between human and nature, independent of all social forms', but 'the labourer can create nothing without nature, without the sensuous (*sinniliche*) external world'. Marx criticised the socialists of his time, like Ferdinand Lassalle, who attributed '*supernatural creative power* to labour' by conceiving it as the sole source of wealth and disregarding the role of nature. He wrote: 'It is false to say that labour insofar as it creates (*hervorbringt*) use values, that is material wealth, is the unique source of the latter.... The use value always has a natural substratum'; 'material wealth, the world of use values, exclusively consists of natural materials modified by labour'. Indeed, judged in physical terms, labour, Marx was wont to observe, could only alter the form of what nature had initially provided. 'Labour', he wrote at the beginning of *Capital,* 'is not the only source of material wealth, of the use-values it produces. As William Petty says, labour is the father of material wealth, and the earth is its mother.'

To be sure, Marx and Engels had little to say about the *absolute* natural limits of the globe. But to claim that Marx failed to take into account natural limits is entirely without foundation. Far from ignoring natural conditions or limits, Marx built them into his analysis of human production, into his conception of nature transcending human production and into his plea for 'associated producers' of the future communist society '*rationally regulating* their interchange with nature.... with the least expenditure of energy and under conditions most favourable to, and worthy of, their human nature'. Marx and Engels would certainly reject ecology's radical division between nature and society, according to which societies face insurmountable natural limits, but their materialist and dialectical theory of the relationship between humanity and nature recognised both the natural limits and constraints inherent in social organisation in any given period. Marx and Engels were indeed unusual in the degree of emphasis they placed on the natural conditions of production, and in their recognition of the fact that a sustainable economy demanded a sustainable relation to nature on a global basis. In this sense, natural limits are very much a part of their argument.

('Limits of nature' is of course an important question and there is the obvious need for us to recognise these limits. However, it also needs to be recognised that to reduce ecological problems to problems of natural limits is to ignore the greater variety of ecological problems – such as pollution and destruction of environment – and their manifold particular causes, and the basic underlying cause in capitalism.)

Although Marx did not concentrate on the ecological critique of capitalism in his writings – no doubt because, as already mentioned, he thought capitalism would be replaced by a society of freely associated producers long before such problems could become truly critical – such critique is a recurring theme in his analysis of capitalist production. Marx defined capitalism as a social system determined by the dynamics of the accumulation of capital. He concluded that it would find its historical limits in the fact that it would erode the two sources of human wealth: the worker (treated as labour power) and nature (treated as inexhaustible). Apropos the latter source of wealth, commenting on Bacon's great maxim that 'nature is only commanded by obeying her', Marx replies that for capitalism the discovery of nature's autonomous laws 'appears merely as a ruse so as to subjugate it under human needs'. He thus decried the one-sided, instrumental and exploitative relation to nature which for him was a necessary part of contemporary capitalist social relations. Writing in the *Grundrisse,* this is how Marx assessed the impact of capitalism on nature, indeed on everything that appeared external to it:

> Just as production founded on capital created universal industriousness on one side.... so does it create on the other side a system of general exploitation of the natural and human qualities, a system of general utility, utilising science itself just as much as all the physical and mental qualities, while there appears nothing *higher in itself,* nothing legitimate for itself, outside this circle of social production and exchange. Thus capital creates the bourgeois society, and the universal appropriation of nature as well as of the social bond itself by the members of society. Hence the great civilizing influence of capital; its production of a stage of society in comparison to which all earlier ones appear as mere *local developments* of humanity and as *nature-idolatry*. For the first time, nature becomes purely an object for humankind, purely a matter of utility; ceases to be recognized as a power for itself; and the theoretical discovery of its autonomous laws appears merely as a ruse so as to subjugate it under human needs, whether as an object of consumption or as a means of production. In accord with this tendency, capital drives beyond national barriers and prejudices as much as beyond nature worship, as well as all traditional, confined, complacent, encrusted satisfactions of present needs, and reproductions of old ways of life. It is destructive towards all of this, and constantly revolutionizes it, tearing down all the barriers which hem in the development of the forces of production, the expansion of needs, the all-sided development of production, and the exploitation and exchange of natural and mental forces. But from the fact that capital posits every such limit as a barrier and hence gets *ideally* beyond it, it does not by any means follow that

> it has *really* overcome it, and since every such barrier contradicts its character its production moves in contradictions which are constantly overcome but just as constantly posited.

Marx saw nature as a 'free gift', something given to capital 'gratis', which is then 'robbed' or 'degraded' by it in the sense that conditions of sustainability, which must take account of the reproduction of nature are violated by capital through its exploitative practices. He early noticed that the bourgeoisie exploits earth or soil on the same basis as every other element of commerce. For the bourgeoisie, he wrote in 1852, 'the soil is to be a marketable commodity, and the exploitation of the soil is to be carried on according to the common commercial laws. There are to be manufacturers of food as well as manufacturers of twist and cottons, but no longer any lords of the land'. Sixties onwards Marx became increasingly concerned about the ecological crisis such exploitation of the soil was giving rise to. Central to his concerns in this respect was the effect of capitalist industrialisation, particularly of capitalist use of science and technology on agriculture, in degrading or exhausting, 'the natural power of the soil'. Marx pointed out the unsustainability of the emerging situation. 'The moral of the tale', he wrote, 'is that the capitalist system runs counter to a rational agriculture, or that a rational agriculture is incompatible with the capitalist system (even if the latter promotes technical development in agriculture) and needs either small farmers working for themselves or the control of the associated producers.' It is this which induced Marx to envision future society of associated producers to a very large extent in terms of sustainability.

Marx identified, under capitalism, the emergence of a metabolic rift brought about by agricultural and trade practices that despoil the earth without replenishing its resources and rob whole regions of their natural conditions of production and reproduction. He noted 'the violation' under capitalist agriculture of 'conditions necessary to lasting fertility of the soil' – of the basic elements of 'the circulation of matter between man and the soil' – through the disruption of the soil nutrient cycle, which called for 'its restoration as a system, as a regulating law of social production, and under a form appropriate to the full development of the human race'. This is what Marx wrote in a well-known passage of *Capital* Vol I:

> Capitalist production by collecting the population in great centres, and causing an ever-increasing preponderance of town population, on the one hand concentrates the historical motive power of society; on the other hand, it disturbs the circulation of matter between man and the soil, i.e., prevents the return to the soil of its elements consumed by man in the form of food and clothing; it therefore violates the conditions necessary to lasting fertility of the soil. By this action it destroys at the same time the health of the town labourer and the intellectual life of the rural labourer. But while upsetting the naturally grown conditions for the maintenance of that circulation of matter, it imperiously calls for its restoration as a system, as a regulating law of social production, and under a form appropriate to the full development of the human race. In agriculture as in manufacture, the transformation of production under the sway of capital, means, at the same time, the martyrdom of the producer; the instrument of labour becomes the means of enslaving, exploiting, and impoverishing the labourer; the social combination and organisation of labour-processes is turned into an organised mode of crushing out the workman's individual vitality, freedom, and independence.... In modern agriculture, as in the urban industries, the increased productiveness and quantity of the labour set in motion are bought at the cost of laying waste and consuming by disease labour-power itself. Moreover, all progress in capitalistic agriculture is a progress in the art, not only of robbing the labourer, but of robbing the soil; all progress in increasing the fertility of the soil for a given time, is a progress towards ruining the lasting sources of that fertility. The more a country starts its development on the foundation of modern industry, like the United States, for example, the more rapid is this process of destruction. Capitalist production, therefore, develops technology, and the combination together of various processes into a social whole, only by sapping the original sources of all wealth – the soil and the labourer.

Thus even as Marx recognised the transhistorical necessity of human dependence upon naturally given conditions, he was aware of the limits to human social activity or its consequences under capitalism. Marx's reference to 'a regulating law' indeed carries with it an explicit advocacy of ecological sustainability, for it is this which would presumably govern socialist agriculture in contrast with its capitalist form.

The argument of the above passage is carried forward by Marx with still greater clarity and sophistication in Volume III of *Capital*, where he again discusses issues of ecological degradation – disruption of the soil nutrient cycle – and restoration and sustainability as a nature-imposed necessity for continued human production. 'Large landed property', he wrote, 'reduces the agricultural production to an ever decreasing minimum and confronts it with an ever growing industrial population crammed together in large towns; in this way it produces conditions that provoke an irreparable rift in the interdependent process of the social metabolism, a metabolism prescribed by the natural laws of life itself. The result of this is a squandering of the vitality of the soil, which is carried by trade far beyond the bounds of a single country.'

Sustainable development has been defined in our time by the Brudtland Commission as 'development which meets the needs of the present without compromising the ability of the future generations to meet their needs'. It was the need for sustainability in precisely this sense that Marx came to emphasise as a result of his research into the crisis of earth or soil under capitalism, and which he posited as an integral part of his conception of a future communist society. Pointing out that capitalism's overriding concern with immediate monetary gain diverts agriculture from its proper purpose of ministering to the permanent human needs, now and in future, Marx wrote: 'The way that the cultivation of particular crops depends on fluctuations in market prices and the constant changes in cultivation with these price fluctuations – the entire spirit of capitalist production, which is oriented towards the most immediate monetary profits – stands in contradiction to agriculture, which has to concern itself with the whole gamut of permanent conditions of life required by the chain of successive generations.'

For Marx, who understood that transcending the ecological contradiction of capitalist agriculture was an absolute necessity for communist society, the question of sustainability was central to the future development of humanity. If earlier, in response to the impairment under capitalism of the metabolic relation between human beings and the earth (or soil), he had argued for its restoration 'as a regulating law of social production, and under a form appropriate to the full development of the human race', Marx now wrote: 'A conscious and rational treatment of the land as permanent communal property, (is) the inalienable condition for the existence and reproduction of the chain of human generations' – precisely what we today refer to as 'sustainable development'.

Sustainability thus understood has obvious revolutionary implications which Marx clearly stated even as he also pointed to the imperative of protecting the earth for future generations. Marx wrote: 'From the standpoint of a higher socio-economic formation, the private property of particular individuals in the earth will appear just as absurd as the private property of one man in other men. Even an entire society, a nation, or all simultaneously existing societies taken together, are not owners of the earth. They are simply its possessors, its beneficiaries, and have to bequeath it in an improved state to succeeding generations, as *boni patres familias* (good heads of the household)'. As Foster has commented: 'Devising a sustainable alternative to the destructive ecological tendencies of capitalist society was thus not merely a technical problem for Marx, but one that required a far-reaching transformation of society. The basic change needed was a shift to a society controlled by the associated producers, characterzied by the expansion of free time and collective-democratic organization, and hence by a non-instrumentalist approach to nature and human society. Among the revolutionary changes necessary to bring this about was an end to "the monopolized earth" of private property. "Private property," Marx contended, referring to James Johnston's analysis of the impoverishment of the soil in the mid-nineteenth century, "places insuperable barriers on all sides to a genuinely rational agriculture."'

It is sometimes contended that Marx addressed ecological problems only in relation to agriculture (the country) and did not consider them also in relation to industry (city or town). This however is a superficial view which fails to understand the dialectical character of Marx's understanding of ecological crises which recognises the development of capitalist agriculture and industry as inextricably interlinked and views the antagonism of town and country under industrial capitalism as integral to the ongoing ecological destruction. Marx had written: 'large-scale industry and industrially pursued large-scale agriculture have the same effect. If they are originally distinguished by the fact that the former lays waste and ruins labour-power and thus the natural power of man, whereas the latter does the same to the natural power of the soil, they link up in the later course of development, since the industrial system applied to agriculture also enervates the workers there, while industry and trade for their part provide agriculture with the means of exhausting the soil'. Again, it was Marx's argument, as we have already noticed, that by agglomeration or 'cramming' the population in large urban centres, capitalism both 'prevents the return to the soil of its elements consumed by man in the form of food and clothing, (and) therefore violates the conditions necessary to lasting fertility of the soil' and 'destroys at the same time the health of the town labourer and the intellectual life of the rural labourer.' This apart, Marx's analysis of capitalism, as we have seen, regularly points to the unintended ecological problems and more direct environmental degradation produced by the exploitative and accumulative logic of capitalism. 'The development of civilisation and industry in general', Marx wrote, 'has always shown itself so active in the destruction of forests that everything that has been done for their conservation and protection is completely insignificant in comparison.'

Marx showed an early awareness of the pollution threat when in his *Economic and Philosophic Manuscripts of 1844*, he referred to 'the universal pollution to be found in large towns'. In such large towns, he wrote, 'Even the need for fresh air ceases to be a need for the worker. Man reverts once more to living in a cave, but the cave is now polluted by the mephitic and pestilential breath of civilisation. Moreover the worker has no more than a precarious right to live in it, for it is for him an alien power that can be daily withdrawn and from which, should he fail to pay, he can be evicted at any time. He actually has to *pay* for this mortuary. A dwelling in the *light,* which Prometheus describes in Aeschylus as one of the great gifts through which he transformed savages into men, ceases to exist for the worker. Light, air, etc. – the simple *animal* cleanliness – ceases to be a need for man. *Dirt* – this pollution and putrefaction of man, the *sewage* (this word is to be understood in its literal sense) of civilisation – becomes an *element of life* for him. Universal *unnatural* neglect, putrefied nature, becomes an element of life for him.'

Marx and Engels indeed saw the division between town and country – a characteristic of capitalist organisation as fundamental to the system as the division between capitalist and labourer – as the source of any number of problems in capitalist society, including its rather serious ecological problems. Hence the importance they accorded to the elimination of this division in their political programme in the *Communist Manifesto* and elsewhere. We have Engels' adjuration in *Anti-Duhring*: 'The present poisoning of the air, water and land can only be put an end to by the fusion of town and country...'

As mentioned earlier, a central theme in Marx's writings, indeed a matter of concern throughout, was humanity's alienation from nature under capitalism. 'The view of nature which has grown up under the regime of private property and of money', Marx wrote, 'is an actual contempt for and practical degradation of nature'. Implicit in this view was the highly estranged relation between man and nature which is a specific feature of capitalism. As Marx saw it, nature originally appears as 'the direct well spring of production' for human beings. Capitalism as a 'regime of private property and of money' breaks this original unity by the alienating character of its mediation between nature and production. The result is an overarching alienation which, according to Marx, 'estranges man' not only from 'himself, his own active functioning', 'his *human essence*' or from other men, but also 'from nature as it exists outside him'. Capitalism presupposes and imposes estrangement between humans and the natural world so that an external instrumental relation between humans and the natural environment displaces an orientation to nature in which human activity is also a source of intrinsic aesthetic, intellectual and spiritual fulfilment. Communism for Marx included restoration to the human species these lost dimensions of their relationship to their non-human natural environment.

Engels shared Marx's understanding of the ecological problems under capitalism as also his overall attitude to nature. Young Engels' *The Conditions of the Working Class in England* was, in effect, a denunciation of the environmental consequences of capitalist industrialisation. About the same time in his first published work on political economy, in 1844, Engels had written: 'To make the earth an object of huckstering – the earth which is our one and all, the first condition of our existence – was the last step toward making oneself an object of huckstering.' And here are two passages from what he wrote towards the end of his life, bearing on the relation of the natural world to human society, passages still fresh in their resonance with the ecological consciousness of our own time:

> As long as the individual manufacturer or merchant sells a manufactured or purchased commodity with the usual coveted profit, he is satisfied and does not concern himself with what afterwards becomes of the commodity and its purchasers. The same thing applies to the natural effects of the same actions. What cared the Spanish planters in Cuba, who burned down forests on the slopes of the mountains and obtained from the ashes sufficient fertiliser for *one* generation of very profitable coffee trees – what cared they that the heavy tropic rainfall afterwards washed away the upper stratum of the soil leaving behind only bare rock! In relation to nature as to society, the present mode of production is periodically concerned only about the immediate, the most tangible result; and then surprise is expressed that the more remote effects of actions directed to this end turn out to be quite different, are mostly quite the opposite in character...'

Again:

> Let us not, however, flatter ourselves overmuch on account of our human conquests over nature. For each such conquest takes its revenge on us. Each of them, it is true, has in the first place the consequences on which we counted, but in the second and third places it has quite different, unforeseen effects which only too often

> cancel out the first. The people who, in Mesopotamia, Greece, Asia Minor, and elsewhere, destroyed the forests to obtain cultivable land, never dreamed that they were laying the basis for the present devastated condition of those countries, by removing along with the forests the collecting centres and reservoirs of moisture. When, on the southern slopes of the mountains, the Italians of the Alps used up the fir forests so carefully cherished on the northern slopes, they had no inkling that by doing so they were cutting at the roots of the dairy industry in their region; they had still less inkling that they were thereby depriving their mountain springs of water for the greater part of the year, making it possible for these to pour still more furious flood torrents on the plains during the rainy season. Those who spread the potato in Europe were not aware that with these farinaceous tubers they were at the same time spreading the disease of scrofula. Thus at every step we are reminded that we by no means rule over nature like a conqueror over a foreign people, like someone standing outside nature – but that we, with flesh, blood, and brain, belong to nature, and exist in its midst, and that all our mastery of it consists in the fact that we have the advantage over all other beings of being able to know and correctly apply its laws.

It may be added that even as Engels pointed out that 'with every day that passes we are learning to understand these laws more correctly, and getting to know both the more immediate and the more remote consequences of our interference with the traditional course of nature', he had also concluded, very much in line with the thinking of Marx that the 'regulation (of) our interference with the traditional course of nature.... requires something more than mere knowledge. It requires a complete revolution in our hitherto existing mode of production, and simultaneously a revolution in our whole contemporary social order.'

XX

A major theme in contemporary ecological debates has been criticism of Marx's so-called 'Prometheanism', wherein he is charged with having a productivist and instrumental, exclusively 'homocentric' or 'anthropocentric' attitude to nature. Odd statements like 'the subjection of Nature's forces to man' or 'the idiocy of rural life' in the *Communist Manifesto* (the correct translation, incidentally, is not 'idiocy' but 'isolation') or references to 'control' 'mastery' or 'domination of nature' elsewhere in his (or Engels') works, his appreciation of the positive aspects of capitalism's productivist achievements or achievements of modern science and technology, torn out of their context or isolated from his work as whole, have been cited to make out a case in support of the charge. Marx's admiration for Aeschylus' *Prometheus Bound* and his attraction to Prometheus as a revolutionary figure of Greek mythology has long been known, and criticism of Marx along the above lines has a long history extending back to the early years of the Cold War. But the accusation that Marx's work contained at its heart a 'Promethean motive' and that this constituted the principal weakness of his entire analysis really took off, eighties onwards, under the influence mainly of Leszek Kolakowski's recently published *Main Currents of Marxism*. Kalakowski saw 'Marx's Prometheanism' reflected in 'his lack of interest in the natural (as opposed to economic) conditions' of human existence and accused him of having fallen prey to simple-minded 'Prometheanism'. Any number of scholars since then, including some otherwise sympethic to him, have condemned Marx for his Prometheanism, his so-called Promethean disregard of nature.

Indeed, if there is a single charge that has served to unify all criticism of Marx in recent decades it is this charge of 'Prometheanism'. Thus, socialist Anthony Giddens has complained of Marx's 'Promethean attitude' which supposedly explains why 'Marx's concern with transforming the exploitative human social relations expressed in class systems does not extend to the exploitation of nature'. Socialist environmentalist Ted Benton has criticised Marx for having adopted 'a "productivist" "Promethean" view of history'. For social ecologist (ecological anarchist) John Clark 'Marx's Promethean.... "man" is a being who is not at home in nature, who does not see the Earth as the "household" of ecology. He is an indomitable spirit who must subject nature in the quest for self-realization.... For such a being, the forces of nature, whether in the form of his own unmastered internal nature or the menacing powers of external nature, must be subdued.' According to liberal Victor Ferkiss, 'Marx's attitude towards the world always retained that Promethean thrust, glorifying the human conquest of nature.' Post-modern environmentalist Wade Sikorski has written: 'Marx.... was one of our age's most devout worshippers of the machine. Capitalism was to be forgiven its sins because.... it was in the process of perfecting the machine.' And so on. The charge of 'Prometheanism' is further supported with other common criticisms: Marx's 'unmistakable anthropocentrism', his failure to recognise the natural limits – where the revolutionary socialist Michael Lowy follows Ted Benton and others with the charge that Marx adopted an 'optimistic "promethean" conception of the limitless development of the productive forces' which was 'totally indefensible' – or Marx's value theory which, we are told, designated labour (power) as the source of all value, thereby denying any intrinsic value to nature, etc.

Our discussion in the preceding sections should make it abundantly clear that this charge of 'Protheanism', or interpretation of whatever Protheanism is indeed there in Marx, is not merely mistaken but a gross misrepresentation of his position. Whatever inadequacies Marx's ecological thinking may otherwise have, he cannot be thus faulted regarding his understanding of human-nature relationship. But since the charge is rather common and persisted with and the issue involved remains subject of much controversy between Marxists and ecologists of various hues, a further, somewhat focussed discussion of Marx's Prometheanism, some repetition of argument notwithstanding, will not be out of place.

The issue involved is the crucially important question of the relationship between human beings and nature. Holding that the Marxist account of historical progress is vitiated by the positive value it accords to human mastery or domination over nature, concerned ecologists have argued that this 'Promethean attitude towards nature' is the cause of all evil, and pleaded for a new, harmonious relationship with nature. They favour a re-enchantment of the world, the development of an ecological ethics, a return to modes of a 'simpler life' – all of which one can certainly sympathise with and uphold. But the rejection of the so-called 'promethean attitude' has invariably led to an ecological fundamentalism, which romanticises and anthropomorphises nature and involves a reverse mastery or domination of nature over humankind, even if the naive discourse of romantic ecologists remains unaware of it. The ecologist gone 'radical' comes to think in terms of a polar opposition between humanity and the natural world and turns critical, in effect even hostile, towards any special emphasis on the needs of human beings. There is 'idealisation of unspoiled nature', and a kind of 'naturalism' or anthropomorphisation of nature takes over which seeks to derive organising principles of society and norms of social life from nature or laws of nature. It is 'nature' from whose standpoint ecological problems must now be defined as well as 'laws of nature' to which all human action must now adapt. This lapse of ecology into a fundamentalist eco-centricism, as I have already suggested, is seriously mistaken and muddled in its understanding of nature – unless, of course, one adopts an entirely mystical view of nature. It is absolutely wrong to identify nature with 'good', and collaterally, technology or human culture as such with 'bad'. The 'natural' is not necessarily harmless or always harmonious or beneficial to man. Nature's so-called balance or equilibrium is not the outcome of any harmonious existence of non-human natural species; as often pointed out, one aspect of nature has certainly been 'red in tooth and claws'. No values or morals are in any way immanent in nature itself. Outside of humans nature simply *is;* it is neither good nor bad, neither moral nor immoral, neither beautiful nor ugly. Morals or values arrive only when humans, born of nature's evolutionary processes, arrive on the scene. Anthropomorphisation of nature has only meant the projection of human notions and inventions, values or standards into the working of nature, which hardly qualifies it as an alternative to anthropocentrism. The plain fact is that it is anthro-pocentrism or homocentrism alone which can provide criteria of how to judge and act. It indeed remains the only viable reference point from which to evaluate and tackle ecological problems. It is this essentially humanist position which Marx upholds and which is dismissed by ecologists as a 'homocentric' or 'Promethean' attitude to nature.

Humanism, as we have noticed in different contexts, is the guiding principle of Marx's critique of capitalism. It is also the principle underlying his approach to the problem of humanity's relationship with nature. Reiner Grundmann – who has written quite perceptively on the subject and is not averse to arguing in defence of what he describes as 'the Promethean model' of Marx – has thus sketched Marx's humanist perspective on 'the ecological problematic' of today:

> Marx thought – along the lines of paragraph 4 of Hegel's *Philosophy of Right* – that the more people transform first nature into second nature, the more they would become masters of their fate. And this is the real core and the ultimate source of motivation for Marx's critique. It is the *humanist* conviction that everything that impinges upon human dignity must be submitted to theoretical criticism and practical obviation. The theme of conscious control over human affairs is thus the Archimedean point from which Marx levels his critique of capitalism (but, also, of earlier modes of production). It is from this point that he derives his *normative* perspective of what a communist society should look like. In the first place it should be a society that institutionlizes conscious human control over its fate. And it is this that informs his evaluation of former and existing modes of production. Most instructive in this respect is the opening chapter of *Capital* volume 1, section 4, where Marx discusses the 'Fetish Character of Commodities and Its Secret'. Marx says that people in the ancient world were governed by the product of their brains (that is, religion), whereas in the modern world they are governed by the products of their hands. Both states of affairs are unworthy of human dignity. This is the reason why Marx, throughout his work, put so much stress on the topic of alienation, reification and fetishism. Capitalism was not only criticized for its poor economic performance, which shows up in economic crises; it was not only criticized because it exploited the workers, but also because it reduced the workers to *slaves*, making them dependent on a system of wage-slavery, and prevented them achieving self-realization. But, likewise, capitalists are also caught in a situation unworthy of their human nature: even if they are better

> off than the workers, they cannot control the aggregate outcome of their actions on the world market. Thus they fear the repercussions of their own behaviour, in much the same way that the primitive feared nature.
>
> I believe that this humanist model still has an important place in any critical project of social, political and philosophical theory. And, significantly for the present argument, it also has a direct bearing on the ecological problematic. For if modern societies are threatened by their own transformation of nature, the above analysis by Marx is applicable.

To reject ecological naturalism and argue for humanity's special position within nature that a humanist perspective postulates is not to in any way pit humans *against* nature. Human beings do indeed live in nature and, in drawing their sustenance from it, may even be said to dominate or master it – every technology, even the safest, forms a part of such domination or mastery. But in so doing, as Engels had insisted, 'we by no means rule over nature like a conqueror over foreign people, like someone standing outside nature'. He had specifically added that 'all our mastering of it consists in the fact that we have the advantage over all other beings of being able to know and correctly apply its laws'. This is how human beings bring nature 'under their common control'. This 'common control' is an integral part of Marx's communist project. But in characterising this future communist society there is no 'triumphalism', or utopianism of the 'productivist' account, in Marx or Engels. Communism, for them, is a state of affairs in which human beings are capable (for the first time) of full self-realisation, because all natural and social conditions of their existence are now the products of their *common conscious control*. In this view communism also means a qualitatively new phase of increasing mastery over nature.

As Grundmann has pointed out, the words 'domination' or 'mastery' must be understood as denoting 'conscious control' in the same sense that we speak of 'taming' a river or of taming wild animals. Or, still better, of 'masterly' play by a musician. Obviously domination of nature does not mean that one behaves in a reckless fashion towards it, any more than we suggest that a masterly player dominates his instrument (say a violin) when he hits it with a hammer. To those who would criticise the concept of 'domination' of nature because of its odd connotations, Grundmann replies by drawing attention to this reflection by Walter Benjamin: 'The mastery of nature, so the imperialists teach, is the purpose of all technology. But who would trust a cane wielder who proclaimed the mastery of children by adults to be the purpose of education? Is not education above all the indispensable ordering of the relationship between generations and therefore mastery, if we are to use this term, of that relationship and not of children? And likewise technology is not the mastery of nature but of the relation between nature and man.'

It does not much help to postulate a pre-given ideal of natural harmony between humankind and nature or entertain romantic visions of an idealistically conceived completely new human relationship with nature. Human living at all times has necessarily involved interchange with and transformation of nature, the appropriate forms of such human insertion in nature being set and defined by evolving human economies and cultures, the historically existing societies as they necessarily deal with nature. To regard such human insertion or dealing with nature (described variously as domination or mastery, manipulation, harnessing or inducting) as in itself the crucial point, the 'cause', so to speak, of ecological problems is simply mistaken. Ecological problems arise only from *specific* ways of dealing with nature. And, as Marxists have argued, the modern environmental crisis has arisen from the specific way of dealing with nature that is capitalism.

Against his critics, it is necessary to remember that Marx was not the only thinker attracted to the Greek myth of Prometheus, who was the predominant cultural hero of the entire Romantic period in Europe, and who stands in western culture not only for technology but even more for creativity, revolution and general revolutionary consciousness, and for rebellion against the gods (against religion). Rubens, Titian, Dante, Milton, Blake, Goethe, Beethoven, Byron, Shelley, and numerous others incorporated Prometheus as a central motif in their work. In Marx's own work Prometheus is invoked more often as a symbol of revolution than as a symbol of technology. For Marx, the Prometheus to be admired is the revolutionary mythical figure of Aeschylus' *Prometheus Bound* who defied the gods of Olympus and brought fire (light, enlightenment) to human beings and not the ecologists' image of Prometheus as a representative of machine or technology, of mastery and control over nature. This other image is entirely absent from Marx's writings except in the context of his critique of the mechanistic Prometheanism of Proudhon, where Marx refers to the 'new Prometheus' of Proudhon as a 'queer character'. There is no denying that Marx, in line with the Enlightenment tradition placed considerable faith in rationality, science, technology, and human progress, and that he often celebrated the growing human mastery over natural forces. But this is far from the kind of mechanistic Prometheanism that is sought to be foisted upon Marx. Such 'Prometheanism' is a feature not so much of Marxism of Karl Marx as of the hegemonic vision of political economy inherited from bourgeois civilisation.

Marx *is* Promethean in his attitude to humanity and nature. But his prometheanism springs from his humanist ethics which accords humans their rightfully special position within nature and is hopefully concerned about their emancipation and self-realisation, the full flowering of their creative powers in future. 'For *man the supreme being is man*', Marx wrote in his *A Contribution to the Critique of Hegel's Philosophy of Right*, adding '*the categorical imperative to overthrow all conditions* in which man is a humiliated, enslaved, despised and rejected being.'

Given *his* Promethean conception of man and, therefore, of the relation between man and nature, Marx of course rejected any 'cult of nature' or 'nature worship', or what he described as 'man's childish attitude to nature'. He made fun of the view where 'man' sees only harmony and happiness in nature – 'Gay flowers', 'tall and stately oaks', 'forest birds' and 'the enjoyment of their lives', etc. In a polemic against the 'true socialists' (in the *German Ideology*) Marx wrote: '"Man" could also observe a great many other things in nature, e.g., the bitterest competition among plants and animals.... he could further observe that there is open warfare between the "forest birds" and the "infinite multitude of tiny creatures".' 'Hobbes', he said, 'had much better reasons for invoking nature as a proof of his *bellum omnimum contra omnes* (war of one against all)'. Marx rejected 'sentimental' notions of nature based on the illusion that nature was still in a pristine condition and could be left untouched. He saw it intertwined with human history and on this ground sharply attacked the romantics of his day who sought to root themselves and society in a conception of unspoiled nature – as an adequate basis for a revolt against capitalism. He would have had little sympathy with what has been described as 'a spontaneous ideology of the late twentieth century – ecological romanticism'.

But Marx equally rejected a mercenary, instrumental or utilitarian attitude to nature. He saw nature as 'man's inorganic body' and man as 'a part of nature'. Even as he wrote of humankind's 'mastery over nature', he also spoke of human 'participation in nature'. 'Subjection of nature's forces to man' went hand in hand with Bacon's famous injunction: 'We can only command Nature by obeying her'. With Marx emphasis was always on the necessary unity of human and natural existence. We cannot overcome natural necessity – we cannot conquer nature; but neither can we ignore the conscious, social, and cumulative character of human production by taking refuge in 'an indealised, unmediated nature that no longer exists.' If Marx argued for socialisation of human production, it was in order for humankind to develop its own rich possibilities for free development *and* realise its essential unity with nature at a higher level, that is, win what Paul Burkett has called 'a real socialisation of nature' – different and divorced from the distorted form that it assumed under the regimes of private property.

A major concern with Marx as we have repeatedly noticed, was overcoming humanity's alienation from nature involved in the distortion of its relation with nature under the regime of private property that is capitalism. Even as it enables us to satisfy our bodily needs, Marx saw non-human nature as a source of spiritual or aesthetic nourishment – 'Just as plants, animals, stones, air, light, etc., constitute theoretically a part of human consciousness, partly as objects of natural science, partly as objects of art – his spiritual inorganic nature, spiritual nourishment which he must first prepare to make palatable and digestible....' Marx criticised capitalism for alienating 'man from man' and 'from himself, his own active functioning.' But he was equally sharp in pointing out that capitalism 'estranges man from nature'. His vision of the non-alienated emancipatory content of the future communist society has, as a central theme, a 'participation in nature' by humankind which makes possible the full development of nature's aesthetic and spiritual dimensions for human beings. Communism is visualised as the 'genuine resolution of the conflict between man and nature and between man and man'. This resolution involves a qualitatively different, aesthetically and spiritually more fulfilling relationship of humankind with nature, whose part it is and in whose midst it lives and survives. In his *Economic and Philosophic Manuscripts of 1844* Marx wrote: 'The *human* essence of nature first exists only for *social man*; for only here does nature exist as the *foundation* for his own *human* existence. Only here has what is to him his *natural* existence become his *human* existence, and nature become man for him. Thus *society* is the unity of being of man with nature – the true resurrection of nature – the naturalism of man and the humanism of nature both brought to fulfilment'. (It may be added that it is this fulfilment, the reconciliation of man and nature, which has been and remains impossible to realise within capitalism).

Marx thus was no crude or mechanistic Promethean that his ecologist critics have tried to make him out to be. More than a mistake, this is to misunderstand the entire thrust of his philosophical-political position, the essential meaning of his life and work. His concern with science and technology, humankind's material progress was subservient to his more basic ethical concern with human liberation and fulfilment, a joyful life for all lived in a transparent and friendly, sustainable relation with nature. In his *All That Is Solid Melts Into Air*, questioning the attribution of crude Prometheanism to Marx, Marshall Berman has written:

> If Marx is fetishistic about anything, it is not work and production

> but rather the far more complex and comprehensive ideal of *development* – 'the free development of physical and spiritual energies' (1844 manuscripts).... Marx wants to embrace Prometheus *and* Orpheus; he considers communism worth fighting for, because for the first time in history it could enable men to have both....

XXI

The question of Prometheanism apart, and evidence to the contrary notwithstanding, Marx has been criticised as a votary of 'technologism'; critics have questioned what they describe as his exaggerated faith in or unqualified celebration of technology and technological progress. Even otherwise, technology by itself has emerged as an issue in the environmental crisis. For many ecologists, even others, it stands at the very heart of the matter – both as the source and solution of the crisis. Technology itself is expected in the end to find a way out of the corner into which it is supposed to have pushed the world. A brief comment on these two issues is therefore in order.

Apropos the issue of technology, as problems endemic to capitalism continue to pile up in society and the dominance of bourgeois ideology prevents people from seeing their systemic basis and interconnections, there is a widely shared belief or hope, even among those who should know better, that 'technology has a solution to every problem'. Accordingly, 'the miraculous agency of that *deus ex machina*, technology' is what many if not most ecologists look to for salvation in ecological matters. The advocates of 'an environmental revolution' indeed argue that we have today the technology needed to save the environment and have sustainable development; the possibilities of technical innovation are immense and the key to the problem lies in changing our production technologies. The argument certainly has a strong point to it in view of the actual and prospective developments in such areas as solar power, organic farming and integrated pest management, recycling trash, pollution control measures, etc. But experience with such technological solutions has only shown up their utter inadequacy in the face of the looming environmental crisis.

Dealing almost invariably with individual or separate problems, their overall impact has been fragmentary and limited, local or temporary, even superficial, and not unoften they have served to enhance bureaucratic power in society. Further, the focus on technology has obviated the need to take a genuinely critical look at the present *system* of production and consumption. There is a lack of recognition of the systemic sources of the environmental problems, which has been, even more significantly, accompanied by ignorance about the social embeddedness of technology. There is the all-too-prevalent assumption that technologies are neutral products of an autonomous process of technological progress so that all we need to do is pick and choose between them, adapt and use those that are environment-friendly and discard those that degrade or destroy the environment. Which is simply not the case. Technology, once it has come up does come to acquire a certain dynamic of its own, but at a deeper level it is oriented by economic and socio-cultural systems of a society. In other words, it is always socially embedded.

In today's context, those who seek ecological salvation in technology need to recognise its embeddedness in the capitalist system and see technological progress as what it really is, a force directed in large measure by the profit motive, often a by-product of the system's search for more effective military operations. In other words, today's technology and technological progress are subject to the economic and political logic of capitalism which is, ecologically and otherwise, necessarily destructive of the environment. Technological enthusiasts believe that their technologies can override the logic and power of capital. There is little evidence, however, to support such a view. Istvan Meszaros has written, '.... to say that "science and technology *can* solve all our problems in the long run" is much worse than believing in witchcraft; for it tendentiously ignores the devastating social embeddeness of present-day science and technology.... the issue (therefore) is not *whether* or *not* we use science and technology for solving our problems – for obviously we must – but whether or not we *succeed* in radically *changing* their *direction* which is at present narrowly determined and circumscribed by the self-perpetuating needs of profit maximisation.' This is an imperative which, as Marx had argued, allows no consideration either for man or nature. Capitalism, in its pursuit of profit, produces and uses technologies that devastate both humanity and environment.

As for the issue of Marx and technology, it is well to remember that in Marx, celebration of the productive achievements of capitalism notwithstanding, there is no celebration of technology *as such*. Recognising science and technology both as part of the growth of generic human knowledge of the world and as the socially determined product of a particular society interpreting and using nature according to its own priorities, Marx saw not only their beneficial effects but also the negative aspects and destructive potential under capitalism. This is a theme to which Marx reverts again and again in his writings. He was well aware of the fact that science and technology could be misused and distorted by capitalism, a form of society which, as he and Engels noted in the *Communist Manifesto*, 'is like the sorcerer, who is no longer able to control the powers of the nether world whom he has called up by his spells'. Marx regularly pointed to the contradictions-laden nature of technology-use under capitalism. Thus:

> In our days, everything seems pregnant with its contrary. Machinery, gifted with the wonderful power of shortening and fructifying human labour, we behold starving and overworking it. The new-fangled sources of wealth, by some strange weird spell, are turned into sources of want. The victories of art seem bought by the loss of character. At the same pace that mankind masters nature, man seems to become enslaved to other men or to his own infamy. Even the pure light of science seems unable to shine but on the dark background of ignorance. All our invention and progress seem to result in endowing material forces with intellectual life, and in stultifying human life into a material force. This antagonism between modern industry and science on the one hand, modern misery and dissolution on the other hand, this antagonism between the productive powers and the social relations of our epoch is a fact, palpable, overwhelming and not to be controverted.

This fact, one may add, is as much a fact of the present situation, where the revolutionary new technologies from computers and lasers to biotechnology and genetic engineering are providing ever more destructive weapons for the military, automation and information technology are destroying jobs, displacing values, degrading society and stunting our culture, and the networked computer is threatening to be constitutive of a new form of capitalism, a crucial element in 'surveillance society' organised for competitive success under capitalism – even as all these technologies are, one way or the other, also serving to swell the profits of the rich and superrich in our society.

More specifically, technology was an important element in Marx's conception of alienation which, for him, has two interrelated aspects. In one aspect alienation in capitalism is a social phenomenon that arises on the basis of commodity production under conditions of private production and markets. In another it occurs at the level of the labour process itself, in relation to the technology or machinery use which Marx saw as degrading, crippling and depriving the workers. Marx wrote: 'Past labour confronts the worker in the form of an automaton moving a machine, apparently autonomous from labour, self-acting. Instead of being subordinated to labour, it subordinates labour, the iron man against the man of flesh and blood. The subordination of his work under capital.... which is already given with the concept of capitalist production, appears here as a technological fact. The keystone is ready. Dead labour endowed with movement, and living labour only existing as one of its conscious organs'. Again: 'It is the machinery which possesses skill and strength, is itself the virtuoso, with a soul of its own.... The workers' activity, reduced to a mere abstraction of activity, is determined and regulated on all sides by the movement of machinery and not the opposite.'

With Marx, this understanding of technology under capitalism reinforced his general argument in favour of socialism. For the answer to the problem of technology, alienation or otherwise, lies in a *socialist* transcendence of capitalism which, in replacing its commodity production, the private pursuit of profit in the market place, with planned production for social use, also establishes producers' and consumers' conscious control over the labour process and use of technology and makes possible the change and replacement of technology born of capitalism, that has a detrimental impact on the natural environment (and also on human beings), by a technology that meets the criteria that it be consciously controlled and worthy of human nature.

This answer, the necessity of conscious social control in matters of technological development and usage, is immediately relevant to the contemporary environmental crisis. It is true, as scientist-ecologist Barry Commoner has said, 'the technological basis for the transformation of the present systems of production to ecologically sound ones is largely in hand'. But there is a fundamental obstacle. As Commoner recognises it: 'such a transformation of the systems of production conflicts with the short-term profit-maximizing goals that now govern investment decisions; and that, accordingly, politically suitable means must be developed that bring the public interest in long-term environmental quality to bear on these decisions'. Putting it even more bluntly he says: 'As we have seen, our reigning ideology, capitalism, clashes with the reality of the environmental crisis – not to speak of the reality of our country's shameful levels of poverty, and our inadequacies in the areas of housing, medical care and education.' (The country referred to is the United States).

The conclusion is obvious: what has to be done to resolve the environmental crisis, hence also to ensure that humanity has a future, is to replace capitalism with a social order based on an economy devoted not to maximising private profit and accumulating ever more capital but rather to meeting real human needs and restoring the environment to a sustainably healthy condition.

In drawing this conclusion it is necessary to reiterate the specificity of socialism in relation to capitalism. From a Marxist standpoint capitalism as a mode of production or a social formation is not to be identified merely with private ownership of the means of production, with the existence of a class of owners in pursuit of their private interests, so that an altruistic social ownership is the solution to our problems. It is an all-embracing social mode of commodity production arising from a particular type of accumulation and reproduction characterised by the precedence it accords to exchange values as against use values, producing an entire network of relationships for human beings, not only more complex and complicated than any in human history, but simultaneously exploitative and alienating, which distort the relation between man and his labour and product, between man and man, and between man and nature as well. Capitalism's in-built attitude towards human beings and nature alike as means to an alien end, equally diminishes and devastates both. But to acknowledge this specificity of capitalism is at the same time to insist upon the specificity of socialism. Socialism is not simply an extension or an improvement upon capitalism, a society that eliminates the most objectionable features of capitalism such as gross inequality of income, mass unemployment, cyclical depressions, financial panics, and so on. Expropriation of capitalists certainly makes possible a planned use of the social surplus available, but socialism is not to be understood merely as a transfer of ownership or planning leading to a more just distribution of wealth while other relationships remain alienated and reified as before. Marx and Engels always conceived socialism as the quintessential *negation* of capitalism. Of course it is a system which is not driven by the imperatives of accumulation and so-called 'growth' with their attendant waste of human and natural resources and destruction of environment, or whose values and creative impulses are not circumscribed by the constricted notions of technological progress. But socialism for Marx and Engels also involves a total revolutionisation of relationship between human beings and their labour and product, between human beings themselves, and between human beings and nature, that is, of the whole social production of their lives.

This is the meaning of the necessary revolutionary change today. Only such a view of transition from capitalism to socialism will allow the ecological problem to be effectively dealt with. Lesser measures of reform, no matter how desirable or welcome in themselves, will not be able to reverse the ongoing degradation and destruction of the environment and save it; they could at best slow down the fatal process of decline and fall that is already so far advanced.

XXII

The environment has been damaged by all social systems, more or less, since at least 15,000 years ago, since the agricultural revolution which brought in class-society, and the civilisation the way we have known it. But four odd centuries of capitalism have transformed the world far more drastically than all the millennia of previous human history combined. With capitalism, especially since the Second World War, the damage to environment has acquired an altogether new frightening dimension which is posing the threat of an imminent ecological disaster. Not a natural process nor the result of economic growth or industrialisation as such, this damage and the accompanying threat have grown directly out of the specific *structural* logic of capitalism. The productive forces which capitalism has unleashed have been caught up with and overtaken by the destructive powers it released simultaneously, and these are now about to break down the highly strained ecological equilibrium, putting a question mark on the very survival of humankind on this earth. As Foster recently put it: 'Human society has reached a critical threshold in its relation to the environment. The destruction of the planet, in the sense of making it unusable for human purposes, has grown to such an extent that it now threatens the continuation of much of nature, as well as the survival and development of society itself.'

The threat has been growing over the years and so have been the warnings, even if its linkages with capitalism have not been always clearly seen. Way back in 1864, George Perkins Marsh – famous environmentalist and 'the fountain-head of the conservative movement' in the words of Lewis Mumford – taking note of the damage already done to environment by 'the operations of causes set in action by man', had warned: 'The earth is fast becoming an unfit home for its noblest inhabitant, and another era of equal human crime and improvidence.... would reduce it to such a condition of impoverished productiveness, of shattered surface, of climatic excess, as to threaten the depravation, barbarism, and perhaps even extinction of the species.' A century later, Rachel Carson saw this threat as 'the central problem of our age' and argued: 'Along with the possibility of the extinction of mankind by nuclear war, the central problem of our age has.... become the contamination of man's total environment with such substances of incredible potential for harm – substances that accumulate in the tissues of plants and animals and even penetrate the germ cells to shatter or alter the very material of heredity upon which the shape of the future depends.' The epigraph for Carson's book, the environmental classic *Silent Spring*, was a quote from Albert Schweitzer: 'Man has lost the capability to foresee and forestall. He will end by destroying the earth.' About a decade later, noting the disastrously negative consequences of capitalism and viewing resistance to capitalism as *the* necessary human defence, in *The City and the Country*, Raymond Williams wrote: 'Capitalism, as a mode of production.... its abstracted economic drives, its fundamental priorities in social relations, its criteria of growth and of profit and loss, (have) over several centuries altered our country and created our kinds of city. In its final form of imperialism it has altered the world.... Resistance to capitalism is the decisive form of the necessary human defence.' More recently referring to five past mass extinctions (in which 65 per cent or more of species died out in a brief geological instant, and the last one saw the decimation of dinosaurs), scientists have been warning that we are on the verge of 'the sixth extinction' – this time at the hands of humanity. According to the 'World Scientists Warning to Humanity' initiated by the Union of Concerned Scientists and signed in 1992 by 1,575 of the world's most distinguished scientists, including more than half of all living scientists awarded the Nobel prize: 'Human beings and the natural world are on a collision course. Human activities inflict harsh and often irreversible damage on the environment and on critical resources. If not checked, many of our current practices put at risk the future we wish for human society and the plant and animal kingdom, and may so alter the living world that it will be unable to sustain life in the manner that we know. Fundamental changes are urgent if we are to avoid the collision our present course will bring'. The World Scientists go on to emphasise 'the critical stress' in such areas as the atmosphere, the oceans, water resources, soil, forests, and living species – 'the irreversible loss of species, which by 2100 may reach one-third of all species now living is especially serious'. Their conclusion is unmistakably clear: 'We the undersigned, senior members of the world's scientific community, hereby warn all humanity of what lies ahead. A great change in our stewardship of the Earth and the life on it is required if vast human misery is to be avoided and our global home on this planet is not to be irretrievably mutilated'. Commenting on a government-funded study on the decline of species – butterflies, birds and plants – in the UK, recently reported in the magazine *Science*, Jeremy Thomas of the National Environment Research Council has said, the data 'adds enormous strength to the hypothesis that the world is approaching its sixth major extinction event'. And finally, stressing the need to fight capitalism before it destroys us and our planet, Paul Buhle has written: 'Today, human society, and the biosphere itself, cannot survive the organised greed and environmental ruination that the system demands for its continued vampire-like existence'.

As we have argued, it is impossible for capitalism to counter the emerging threat to environment within its own parameters as an economic system. For a capitalism in crisis as it is today (recession, stagnation in economy, unemployment, etc.) it is doubly impossible. Retreating even from their earlier, mostly verbal, concern for the environment, the governmental and political leaders of global capitalism have made it clear (at international conferences and elsewhere) that they will not allow environmental controls to interfere with or 'hurt' the economy, that their only efficient concern is to keep capitalism going, and the environment be damned. They would rather defend and uphold the global capitalist interests, carry on with their consumerist, privileged way of life and shift the immediate pollution and environmental degradation from wealthy areas to poor areas within their own countries and from the advanced capitalist world to its peripheries in the third world. Notwithstanding their cynical use of ecological concern to hinder economic development in countries of the third world in the name of 'global interdependence', or otherwise gain advantage over them in the world market, they fail to see that environmental crisis recognises no barriers within or without, that for it, it is no longer first, second, third or fourth worlds but only one world. This short-sightedness has been compounded by capitalism's recharged domination of the world, following the collapse of the Soviet Union, which has given rise to an era of privatisation and the market-knows-best-solution to all socio-economic problems. Rather than increase regulation and enforcement to reduce pollution or check ecological degradation, the strategy of dominant capitalist powers is to set up a worldwide 'free market', their dominion in which multinationals can freely buy and sell the right to pollute and further degrade the environment. Such dominance of the market in a period of economic crisis can ultimately lead only to an ecological disaster.

There are those who believe 'ultimately' means so far in the future, like the cooling of the sun, as to be for all practical purposes irrelevant. But those who know, reputable ecologists, environmentalists and scientists, have warned us that we are already on the brink of this disaster. Some ten years back an article in the reputed magazine *Natural History*, writing of a 'throw away society' which is 'strangling itself', had reported: 'if the world is not to fatally overtax its natural systems, we will need to achieve sustainability within the next forty years. If we have not succeeded by then, environmental deterioration and economic decline are likely to be feeding on each other, pulling us into a downward spiral of social disintegration. Our vision of the future therefore looks to the year 2030'. About the same time, pointing out that 'the global environment is what sustains us and in some ways we are the villains and victims of the changing environment,' and that what lay ahead was droughts all over the planet, conflict over water resources, massive flooding of coastal cities, disappearance of entire Bangladesh and so on, the eminent scientist late Carl Sagan had warned that human society faced disaster by the year 2050, if it did not change to a more life sustaining technology or development. A recent secret Pentagon report warns of much the same, of climate change over the next 20 odd years causing a global catastrophe – mega-droughts, famines, nuclear threat and wars to defend and secure dwindling food, water and energy supplies, major European cities sunk beneath rising seas and parts plunged into a 'Siberian' climate. Lester Brown, currently president of Earth Policy Institute, even as he continues to look for solutions within the system (and collect awards) fears that 'time is running out for us', that 'we are losing the war to save the planet'. Oliver S. Laud, Professor of Physical Sciences at Antioch University has written: 'On this, *our* planet, there have been about 1000 human generations since our species survived alone among several hominid species, to become *the* culture-creating species. And only the last 200 generations have been born into hierarchical, class-structural social systems. Five generations, three of them already here will either win or lose forever the human future.'

Forty to fifty years or a couple more generations may be too short a period and we need not be alarmist. Such warnings may only indicate the need for an all-sided struggle against the destructive tendencies of our existing social order which today are in full operation. Even so, environmental destruction can no longer be viewed as a long-run problem. In these opening years of the twenty-first century, we can no longer afford the luxury of continuing to think in terms of traditional historical time. From an ecological point of view the human species is indeed in deep trouble today. If things continue to develop as they have over the last fifty years for another century or two – a very short time by historical standards – it is virtually certain that civilized life as we know it today will no longer be possible. Unless we succeed in getting rid of capitalism within a hundred years, the end of human history may be actually not a bad dream, or the poor concoction of a Fukuyama, but a reality.

We indeed do not have much time. As Sara Parkin,

spokesperson of the U.K. Green Party has observed: 'Our numbness, our silence, our lack of outrage, could mean we end up the only species to have minutely monitored our own extinction. What a measly epitaph that would make – they saw it coming but hadn't the wit to stop it happening'. 'There is no guarantee of human tenure on earth' according to Carl Sagan. About 65 million years ago dinosaurs ruled the earth. 'They are extinct. This is a reminder to us to be careful'. Alfred North Whitehead, one of the greatest thinkers of this past century, had written: 'I have never ceased to entertain the idea that the human race might rise to a certain point and then decline and never retrieve itself. Plenty of other forms of life have done that. Evolution may go down as well as up'. It is an unsettling but by no means a far-fetched thought that the form and active agency of this decline may be taking shape before our very eyes in these opening years of the twenty-first century A.D.

This is no 'environmental apocalypticism' or 'millenarianism', or 'doomsday' prophecy, as some critics have alleged. The terms used by critics, 'apocalyptic', 'millenarian' or 'doomsday', because of the sense of religious fatalism associated with them, imply something irrational in character – the wrath of God, the second coming, Day of Judgement – which it should be obvious, has nothing to do with our argument. Our argument carries no suggestion of any kind of uncontrollable destruction of earth's natural conditions. What is suggested is that if humanity constructs a kind of society that systematically destroys the natural ground of its own existence then it is heading for a disaster. Or, to put it more specifically, if our society continues to be dominated by capitalism, then it is only a matter of time – be it a few decades or a few centuries, neither of which amounts to much in the long stretch of history – before it expires from lack of essential life supports. It is not apocalyptic to warn about the disastrous dimensions that capitalism's threat to environment has now acquired.

This however is not the only threat looming on the horizon – the possible parting gift of capitalism to humankind. In yet another way the great capitalist powers, the overlords of contemporary bourgeois civilisation, with their accumulation of high-tech arms and arsenals of nuclear and chemical weapons, are proving incapable of a responsible stewardship of the world's affairs. David Edgerton has spoken of a 'liberal militarism' of the west, long exemplified by the U.S. and British military policy, that today aims at the imposition of a global 'Pax Technologica', based on deployment of high-tech strike forces. This 'liberal militarism' achieves a distinctive fusion of economics and warfare, technology and globalism, with the 'new imperialism' that a Blair has even decreed necessary, recycling the synoptic-warfare delusions of the 'old colonialism'. At the head of this 'new imperialism' stands the United States, with its long record of military interventions, regional wars, counter-revolutionary subversions, low-intensity conflicts and proxy wars the world over–since the second half of the 1940s alone, in China, Korea, Greece, Vietnam, Iran, Guatemala, Middle East, Cuba, Dominican Republic, Chile, Grenada, Nicaragua, Afghanistan, Angola, El Salvador, Iraq and so on, invariably in order to either maintain or restore the status quo, or to pursue its imperialist interests. The 1992 Iraq war, which was obviously not the last of the imperialist interventions – it has already been followed by the war on Afghanistan and another war on Iraq – was significant in more ways than one. It secured the U.S. domination in the strategically important Middle East with its oil reserves which fuel the consumerist extravagance of the west – just as its recent war on Afghanistan has secured for it an assured military presence and political domination in yet another strategically important and oil-rich region of the world, something it has been wanting for a long time. It also exposed the fragile ecology of the Gulf to the pyrotechnics of modern warfare – as has again happened with America's recent wars in the region and beyond. Particularly significant, however, was the belief or the false presumption it generated about the demise of 'the Vietnam syndrome' – America had won a war in the third world along with an assurance for the Americans that they can henceforth kill others but need no longer themselves die in the imperialist interventions abroad. Thus emboldened, and as the world's sole superpower, America has gone altogether adventurist in pursuit of its imperialist aims. It has claimed the right to pre-emptive strike, to unilateral, at-will armed intervention wherever it wants. As an imperial power it has world's largest stock of weapons of mass destruction and proposes to have more of them – including those which are 'about blowing people up on the other side of the planet even if no country on earth will allow us to use their territory' – and its politics is not immune to Bushite 'make-no-mistake' 'greatest nationism' and the itch to bomb recalcitrant nations 'into the parking lot,' to its being a rogue, even 'terrorist state' in Chomsky's words, which it indeed is today in its so-called 'war against terrorism'. However messy, politically and militarily, they may have turned out to be, through its wars on Iraq and Afghanistan, the United States has virtually served notice to people in the third world that imperialist domination is a fate that must be accepted on pain of violent destruction. The people of the third world may, and are likely to defy and reject this notice. But this does not rule out the possibility that, with its short-run vision and arrogance as well as impotence of power, and long record of imperialist interventions, the U.S. may yet, in the words of Paul Sweezy, come 'to play Samson in the temple of humanity'.

This is not to suggest that either irreversible evolutionary decline or military destruction of human species is inevitable. In human affairs nothing is really inevitable until it happens. But capitalism today has a deadly potential for both.

XXIII

Let me conclude by putting the argument in a historical perspective. Marx assessed the significance of capitalism in the development of mankind as creating the conditions for socialism. He visualised the construction of socialism on the basis provided by the productive and other achievements of capitalism. He saw socialism as necessary and possible but not as a smooth and unproblematic transition. There was no assumption that different countries involved in *socialist transition* would all actually exhibit a determinate degree of approximation to the socialist goal on a linear scale. Nor was this transition seen as in any sense inevitable. Decisive here was political intervention that immediately Marx defined as 'proletarian revolution' – which, again, Marx certainly regarded as a necessary but not an automatic and inevitable, or necessarily violent, consequence of capitalist development. Proletarian revolution has remained delayed in the advanced capitalist countries, and where it occurred, as in Germany in 1918, it did not survive. And where it survived, as in Russia in 1917, there were hardly any achievements of capitalism to build upon. The effort to build socialism there has now finally collapsed. Again this was possible but not inevitable. The post-revolutionary theoretical and political intervention was simply inadequate to cope with the unanticipated task. They could have built better and socialism could have survived, even if not as ideally conceived by Marx, but certainly with long-term possibilities of significant approximation to the ideal. Not inevitable, this first experiment in socialism has yet failed, which leaves capitalism very much 'over-developed', surviving much beyond the period of its historical legitimacy, with consequences now all too visible in the materially, morally, mentally and culturally sick societies of the capitalist world. The entire world, the developed capitalist countries no less, are paying the price for the revolution that never happened in the West and the 'socialism' that has now failed in the East. None of this however in any way falsifies the theory of Karl Marx. He always maintained that there are alternatives in history, and the alternative facing the world today, the advanced capitalist societies no less than others, was long ago expressed by Rosa Luxemburg in the formula: 'either socialism or a descent into barbarism'. The emerging ecological catastrophe has only added to the meaning and the urgency, and the scope, of this statement. The real problem here is not the fact of pollution, the scarcity of resources or overpopulation, but the extent to which a world dominated by capitalist imperatives is able to tackle them. On this account, there is room here only for pessimism. Marx foresaw capitalism as carrying within itself the possibility of 'the total destruction of humanity', and also noted: '*Apre moi le deluge*! is the watchword for every capitalist and every capitalist nation'. That is how capitalism is ruining the human habitat and will continue to do so as long as it exists. It is an open question how far the destruction which it has wrought and continues to wreak is still reversible. But given the tenacity with which the capitalist mode of production still asserts itself, it seems certain that in another hundred years or so, maybe less, we will be beyond the point of no return. The fight against capitalism has become a race with time which mankind is in danger of losing.

But the fight is not yet lost. Capitalism certainly holds no possibility of realising Marx's project for the reconciliation of man and nature. But we can still fight and win against capitalism to realise it, to ensure that 'our sun continues to radiate stably into our cherished biosphere' for the posterity, which could well comprise 200 million more human generations. Concern for the future is indeed what has always provided perspective for and inspired the commitment of revolutionaries. So it has to in our struggle to save the environment.

Winning against capitalism means winning socialism, that is, winning conscious rational control of humanity's metabolism with nature. It is to win our freedom 'in the realm of necessity' as Marx called it, which capitalism by its very nature denies us, and which, to repeat Marx again, 'can only consist in this, that socialised man, the associated producers, govern the human metabolism with nature in a rational way, bring it under their collective control instead of being dominated by it as a blind power, accomplishing it with the least expenditure of energy and in conditions most favourable to, and worthy of, their human nature'.

It is not claimed that socialism offers an instant solution to the problems which confront our planet. But its rejection of capitalist imperatives and drives offers a chance that the problems would be tackled with all the determination that is required. Socialism is no guarantee of salvation, ecological or any other, but there is no other *possibility* of salvation today. At the beginning of the twenty-first century, the choice still remains as, following Marx, Rosa Luxemburg formulated it: 'either socialism or a descent into barbarism'.

Years ago, the French students in their May-June uprising of 1968 expressed this sharp contrast of alternatives magnificently in their slogan: 'Be practical! Do the impossible!' Marcuse had suggested that the new generation that faces the next (that is, twenty-first) century needs to add to this demand 'the more solemn injunction: If we don't do the impossible, we shall be faced with the unthinkable!' The 'unthinkable' today is more than mere 'descent into barbarism'. What is at stake is the actual existence of the world, and with it of the human species. And the task, as eco-feminist Francoise d'Eaubonne, paraphrasing Marx has said, is 'to change the world.... so that there can still be a world'. Socialism is precisely the changed world we need. Once a promise of liberation, socialism has now become a question of survival too. Human species needs socialism not only to realise its potentials but even to survive. That is how the chances of survival and realisation of the potentials of both human species and socialism have come to be interlinked today. Which also means that the future of socialism is as bleak or bright as that of humankind.

Index

Afghanistan 147, 148
African-American and Latino communities 61
agricultural productivity, declining 32
agricultural revolution 141
agricultural techniques 80
air pollution 33, 79
America 147
American way of life 37
Angola 147
anthropocentric – biocentric distinction 86
anti-state hysteria 69
Arizona 31
artificial nature 33
Asia's carbon dioxide 32
Asia's emissions of greenhouse 32

Bacon's famous injunction 133
Bangladesh 32, 144
barbarism 141
Benjamin, Walter 130
Benton, Ted 109, 110, 127
Berman, Marshall 134
bio-regionalism 71
biodiversity 33
bombs 27
Brazil 30, 31, 40, 92
Brown, Lester 88, 145
Buhle, Paul 143
Bush Sr., George 87
Business Council for Sustainable Development 73

capitalism 35, 39, 46, 47, 49, 50-53, 56, 60, 70, 71, 75-76, 78, 81, 83-85, 87, 91, 93-95, 97, 98, 107, 108, 123, 143, 149, 150
  abolition of 57
  defensive actions against 88
  Global 54
  historical specificity of 48
  objectionable features of 140
  structural logic of 55
  long-standing 62
  policies on environment 60
capitalist countries 67
capitalist market economy 45, 94
capitalist relations 57
capitalist system 48, 55, 67
carbon dioxide 58, 65
Carson, Rachel 54, 141-142
Castro, Fidel 61
Central Asian countries 32
chemical and biological

weapons 62
chemical fertilisers 29
chemical hazards 64
Chile 31, 147
China 32, 58, 92, 147
Chinese 37
Chomsky, Noam 50
words of 148
Clark, John 127
class exploitation 69, 84
class-divided societies 60
class-exploitative systems 68
climate change 31, 95, 144
Cold War 28, 126
Commoner, Barry 57, 79, 97, 139
Communism 112, 134
conservation practices 46
conspicuous consumerism 58
consumer culture 58
consumerism 36, 37, 71, 77
mindless 60
consumerist life style 58
crisis-management 78
Cuba 107, 147
Czech Republic 92, 97

deep ecology 71
deforestation 70
degradation and collapse 94
depravation 141
development 61
disease-stricken corals 32
Dominican Republic 147
droughts 95
drugs and pesticides, exporting 66
DuPont, chemical giant 89, 92

Earth Summit 40, 41, 43, 56
eco-feminism 71
eco-friendly manner 72
eco-homo dualism 87
ecological 95
attitude 77
balance 52
crisis 44, 45, 54, 84, 95, 118
and capitalism 70
damage 98
degradation 71, 79, 86
destruction 60, 122
dimension 70
disaster 42, 144
effects 46
fundamentalism 128
hubris 86
movement 84
problems 80, 86, 87, 131
programme 95
project 42
protest 78
radicalism 81
rationality 72, 83, 84
ravages 62
resources 91
romanticism 133
salvation 136
sustainability 119
systems 80
values 77
ecology and environment 72
ecology, politics of 74
economic crisis 54
economic development 38, 44
economic liberalisation 38
economic reductionism 47
ecosystems in Canada 30
ecosystems, natural 33
Edgerton, David 146
education 60
El Salvador 147
Engels 52, 104, 105, 108-112, 116, 123, 124, 125, 130, 140
ecological thinking of 113

England 46
environment industry 93
environment movement 85
environment-friendly
technologies 68
environment-protection
measures 70
environmental
action, agenda of 39
activism 40
colonialism 64, 66
consciousness 45
consciousness 72, 76
crisis 28, 34, 36, 38, 39, 45, 49, 51, 52, 56, 57, 60, 64, 69, 79, 94, 131, 144
contemporary 47
degradation 29, 38, 45, 47, 64, 70, 76, 86
political economy of 85
depredations 100
destruction 63, 83, 96
deterioration 144
injury 42
market 92
movement 41, 72
main-stream 89
politics 67
pollution 91
problems 38, 69, 87, 88, 95
protection 100
protection agencies 36
racism 61
reformers 89
rehabilitation 71
safety demands 57
technologies 92, 93
threat 70
toxins 46
environmentalism 48, 69, 76, 79, 84, 87, 88
conventional 48
mainstream 81
positive achievements of 101
environmentalist movement 74, 75, 76
environmentalist pressure 88
Enzensberger, Hans Magnus 77
Europe 97
feudal 45
exploitation 62
of natural and social wealth 81
of the soil 118

fast foods 37
Ferkiss, Victor 127
first world countries 58, 60, 61
floods and famines 95
foreign funding 41
foreign-funded NGOs 69
fossil fuels 34, 58, 65
Foster, John Bellamy 100, 113, 141
fundamental contradiction 49
fundamental structural change 72
funding agency 40

Germany 148
Giddens, Anthony 127
global capitalism 62, 65, 66, 69, 102
global capitalist system 27
global economy 43, 63
global environment 54, 60, 62, 81
Global Environment Facility (GEF) 35
global environmental crisis 65
global problem 69
global revolution 43
global survival 44
global warming 34, 60, 95

global warming, solution of 65
globalisation 38
globalised elites 69
Gorz, Andre 87
Greece 147
Greek myth of Prometheus 131
Greek mythology 126
green harassment 69
Green movement 74, 85
  contemporary 84
Green parties 74
green-blue film 36
greenhouse effect 34, 65
Greenpeace 42
Grenada 147
Grundmann 130
Guatemala 147
Gulf 147
Gulf war 63

harmful technologies 54
hazardous waste dumps 29, 61, 89
health 60
  status 29
Hippocratic medical ethics 68
Hiroshima 27
human actions 95
human arrogance 86
human beings 57
human health 32
human intervention 47
human needs 49, 50, 57
human values 56, 67

immunisation programmes 68
imperialism 70
  classic pattern of 68
imperialist expansion 62
imperialist warfare 63
India 58, 92
individualism, glorification of 69
industrial 32
  capitalism 103
  sectors 41
industrialisation 71
Intergovernmental Panel on Climate Change (IPCC) 31
Iran 147
Iraq 147, 148

Johnston, James 121
junk culture 69
junk food 69

Karliner, Joshua 63
Kazakhstan 32
  huge grasslands of 32
Kolakowski, Leszek 126
Korea 147
Kovel, Joel 49

Labon, Victor 57
Lassalle, Ferdinand 115
Laud, Oliver S. 145
LDCs (less developed countries) 66
Leiss, William 113
Lenin 100
life-denying 33
life-sustaining 33
lifestyle 65
  throw-away 58
living standards 37
Lunacharsky 100

Machiavellian 68
Macpherson 55
Mahler, Halfdan 68
mainstream environmentalism, weakness of 72
Malay World 63
Malaysia 30, 64
Maldives 32

Mao's words 69
Marsh, George Perkins 141
Martin, Jean 68
Martin Khor Kok Peng 59
Marx, Karl 44, 48, 51-53, 55, 62, 103-105, 106, 109-111, 114-118, 120-123, 127, 128, 130, 133, 134, 138, 140, 148, 149, 151
  and technology 137
  attitude 127
  communist project 130
  critique of capitalism 129
  ecological thinking 127
  ecology 113
  Marxism of 132
  prometheanism of 85, 128
  understanding of the ecological problems 124
Marxian theory 47
Marxism 83, 97, 99, 102-104, 106, 109, 110
  classical 103, 108
Marxist account of historical progress 128
Marxist case, traditional 96
Marxist perspective 102
Marxist terms, classical 98
Meszaros, Istvan 55, 74
Mexico 92
Middle East 147
militant NGOs 41
minorities 60
Montgomery 92
Moscow 101
multinational corporations 73
Mumford, Lewis 141

Nagasaki 27
natural environment 52
natural resource-based activities 46
New Guinea 31
Nicaragua 63, 147
  under Sandinista leadership 107
Non-Governmental Organisations (NGOs) 36, 40, 41, 89, 92
non-polluting technologies 80
Nuclear Missile Defence 28
nuclear weapons 27

O'Connor, James 53
Ozone layer depletion 34

Pacific Islands 32
Parkin, Sara 145
pesticides 29
petrochemical biocides 31
petroleum pollution 70
Petty, William 116
Poland 92
Polanyi, Karl 53
political power 69
polluted air 97
polluted water 97
pollutes and ravages 60
polluting industries 65, 66, 67, 88
polluting technologies 60
pollution 66, 93
  and global warming 54
poor countries 37
poor nations, exploitation of 39
population growth 38, 39
  in the South 39
Post-decolonisation 68
Post-Soviet collapse 69
poverty 39, 69
Pratt, Larry 91, 92
privatisation 144
Proletarian revolution 148
Prometheanism 132
  question of 135

of Proudhon 132
Prometheus, ecologists' image of 132

Quaini, Massimo 113

radical minority 71 ,
radical systemic change 76
Rainforest Action Network (RAN) 63
rational and environmentally benign technologies 68
rational ecological and social order 83
rationality 83, 96
regional planning 52
rehydration therapy 68
rich countries 37
Rio Summit 61, 89
Roman and Mayan civilisations 45
romantic ecologists 128
romantic primitivism 85
Rome 101
rural and urban poor worldwide 60
rural labourer 119
Russia 149

Sagan, Carl 144
Schweitzer, Albert 142
World War Second 27
Sikorski, Wade 127
Smith, Adam 56
social ecology 71
socialism 35, 83-85, 97, 100, 101, 103, 107, 151
for Marx and Engels 140
socio-economic problems 144
socio-economic system 71
South East Asia 32
South Korea 92
Soviet ecology 100
Soviet planning 87
Soviet Union 28, 97, 98, 99, 101, 144
environmental failure in the 98
spiritual powers 49
Stalin 100
sulphur dioxide emissions 32
Sumerian civilisation 45
Sustainable development 38, 42, 43, 44, 60, 61, 73, 95, 120, 135
sustainable economic development 96
sustainable growth 52
Sweezy, Paul 148

third world countries 36, 40, 58, 61-63, 68
colonial and neo-colonial ravaging of 64
poor people of the 60
Third World Network 59
toxic wastes 33, 65, 67, 70
dumps 64
treat bio-diversity 34
tropical deforestation 34

UK 143
UK Green Party 145
UN bodies 36
United Nations 40
United States 41, 56, 58, 59, 60, 61, 62, 65, 92, 97, 147, 148
and British military policy 146
business 59
domination 147
population 37
war against Vietnam 62
unsustainable pattern 38
Uzbekistan 31

Vernadsky 100
Vietnam 147
Vietnam syndrome 147
vulnerable sections 60

wage stream 67
wars 148
wars on Iraq and Afghanistan 63
water, bottled 91
water pollution 32
water refugees 32
Whitehead, Alfred North 146
William Vogt 59
women 60
working class struggles 75
working classes 60
World Bank 35, 40, 42, 66, 88
  warning of, 33
world energy 58
World Trade Organisation (WTO) 92
World War II 57, 101, 141
World Watch Institute 36, 37, 59
World Watch reports 77

Young, John 59

Zero Population Growth 59